Duke University
Durham, North Carolina

Written by Margaret Campbell
Edited by Jessica Pecsenye

Additional contributions by Adam Burns,
Omid Gohari, Christina Koshzow, Chris Mason,
Jon Skindzier, Tim Williams, Joey Rahimi,
Luke Skurman and Kristen Burns

COLLEGE PROWLER

ISBN # 1-59658-044-5
ISSN # 1551-0382
© Copyright 2005 College Prowler
All Rights Reserved
Printed in the U.S.A.
www.collegeprowler.com

Special thanks to Babs Carryer, Andy Hannah, LaunchCyte, Tim O'Brien, Bob Sehlinger, Thomas Emerson, Andrew Skurman, Barbara Skurman, Bert Mann, Dave Lehman, Daniel Fayock, Chris Babyak, The Donald H. Jones Center for Entrepreneurship, Terry Slease, Jerry McGinnis, Bill Ecenberger, Idie McGinty, Kyle Russell, Jacque Zaremba, Larry Winderbaum, Paul Kelly, Roland Allen, Jon Reider, Team Evankovich, Julie Fenstermaker, Lauren Varacalli, Abu Noaman, Jason Putorti, Mark Exler, Daniel Steinmeyer, Jared Cohon, Gabriela Oates, Tri Ad Litho, David Koegler, Glen Meakem, and **the Duke Bounce Back Team.**

College Prowler™
5001 Baum Blvd.
Suite 456
Pittsburgh, PA 15213

Phone: (412) 697-1390, 1(800) 290-2682
Fax: (412) 697-1396, 1(800) 772-4972
E-mail: info@collegeprowler.com
Website: www.collegeprowler.com

College Prowler™ is not sponsored by, affiliated with, or approved by Duke University in any way.

College Prowler™ strives faithfully to record its sources. As the reader understands, opinions, impressions, and experiences are necessarily personal and unique. Accordingly, there are, and can be, no guarantees of future satisfaction extended to the reader.

© Copyright 2005 College Prowler. All rights reserved. No part of this work may be reproduced or transmitted in any form or by any means, including but not limited to, photocopy, recording, or any information storage and retrieval systems, without the express written permission of College Prowler™.

Welcome to College Prowler™

During the writing of College Prowler's guidebooks, we felt it was critical that our content was unbiased and unaffiliated with any college or university. We think it's important that our readers get honest information and a realistic impression of the student opinions on any campus — that's why if any aspect of a particular school is terrible, we (unlike a campus brochure) intend to publish it. While we do keep an eye out for the occasional extremist — the cheerleader or the cynic — we take pride in letting the students tell it like it is. We strive to create a book that's as representative as possible of each particular campus. Our books cover both the good and the bad, and whether the survey responses point to recurring trends or a variation in opinion, these sentiments are directly and proportionally expressed through our guides.

College Prowler guidebooks are in the hands of students throughout the entire process of their creation. Because you can't make student-written guides without the students, we have students at each campus who help write, randomly survey their peers, edit, layout, and perform accuracy checks on every book that we publish. From the very beginning, student writers gather the most up-to-date stats, facts, and inside information on their colleges. They fill each section with student quotes and summarize the findings in editorial reviews. In addition, each school receives a collection of letter grades (A through F) that reflect student opinion and help to represent contentment, prominence, or satisfaction for each of our 20 specific categories. Just as in grade school, the higher the mark the more content, more prominent, or more satisfied the students are with the particular category.

Once a book is written, additional students serve as editors and check for accuracy even more extensively. Our bounce-back team — a group of randomly selected students who have no involvement with the project — are asked to read over the material in order to help ensure that the book accurately expresses every aspect of the university and its students. This same process is applied to the 200-plus schools College Prowler currently covers. Each book is the result of endless student contributions, hundreds of pages of research and writing, and countless hours of hard work. All of this has led to the creation of a student information network that stretches across the nation to every school that we cover. It's no easy accomplishment, but it's the reason that our guides are such a great resource.

When reading our books and looking at our grades, keep in mind that every college is different and that the students who make up each school are not uniform — as a result, it is important to assess schools on a case-by-case basis. Because it's impossible to summarize an entire school with a single number or description, each book provides a dialogue, not a decision, that's made up of 20 different topics and hundreds of student quotes. In the end, we hope that this guide will serve as a valuable tool in your college selection process. Enjoy!

OMID GOHARI ○ CHRISTINA KOSHZOW ○ CHRIS MASON ○ JOEY RAHIMI ○ LUKE SKURMAN ○
Founders of College Prowler™

DUKE UNIVERSITY
Table of Contents

By the Numbers............................ **1**	Drug Scene................................ **99**
Academics **4**	Campus Strictness **103**
Local Atmosphere **12**	Parking...................................... **107**
Safety and Security **20**	Transportation **112**
Computers.................................. **26**	Weather **119**
Facilities..................................... **32**	Report Card Summary **124**
Campus Dining.......................... **37**	Overall Experience **125**
Off-Campus Dining **46**	The Inside Scoop..................... **130**
Campus Housing **52**	Finding a Job or Internship **134**
Off-Campus Housing................ **60**	Alumni Information................. **136**
Diversity..................................... **65**	Student Organizations............ **138**
Guys and Girls **71**	The Best & Worst..................... **143**
Athletics..................................... **77**	Visiting Campus....................... **145**
Nightlife..................................... **85**	Words to Know........................ **149**
Greek Life **93**	

Introduction from the Author

Admitting I go to Duke is sometimes hard—not because I'm ashamed of my school, but because I'm aware of the many naïve people who seem to have no idea what a great university it is. Many know it's in the East, but it's a rare person who can place it in North Carolina. Those who are familiar with Duke most often have been touched by its greatest emissary: Basketball. "Duke? You don't look tall enough to play basketball!" Yeah, that one wears on you after a while. These people should be informed that (at Duke) there is, in fact, life outside of March, and not every Duke student affiliates him or herself with the Cameron Crazies. I must admit though, that I have come to love joining everyone in the dorm commons room for all the away games. A note to readers: prior to enrolling at Duke University, I never sat through a whole basketball game.

Sports fanatic or not, Duke can and will meet your needs in all aspects of the college experience. In a recent national college poll, Duke was ranked number four in overall academics, just behind Princeton, Harvard, and Yale, and tied with Stanford. So, it's safe to say that Duke's keeping some pretty good company academically. Even more so, the university is fun, laid-back, and deeply entwined in its Southern roots. I was raised in the South, and I'd been longing to go back for a long time. Now, don't get me wrong—Duke is an internationally diverse campus. People come from all over the world, and this diversity is a cherished part of the Duke community. However, the weather, the accents, and the easy-going attitudes proclaim that, though this school will continue to grow in many ways, it has yet to lose its roots.

Most of this you must already know. If you're researching colleges you've probably already come across rankings, descriptions of campus and admissions and financial aid statistics. This book may give you a lot more of the same, but that is not exactly its aim. You will find more information about Duke than I ever knew existed before writing this book. There are some vital questions about everyday life answered here, and more importantly, a lot of student opinions have been revealed. So it's best to take what you can find. If you're looking to spend the next four years of your life here, then you have every right to know how "real" Duke students feel about their school. This book will give you this information and then some.

Good luck in your college hunting—and when the admissions letters come in, you should celebrate - and then feel free to thank College Prowler for making your decision that much easier.

Margaret Campbell, Author
Duke University

By the Numbers

General Information

Duke University
Durham, NC 27708

Control:
Private

Academic Calendar:
Semester

Religious Affiliation:
Methodist

Founded:
1838

Website:
www.duke.edu

Main Phone:
(919) 684-8111

Admissions Phone:
(919) 684-3214

Student Body

Full Time Undergraduates:
6,169

Part Time Undergraduates:
79

Total Male Undergraduates:
3,198

Total Female Undergraduates:
3,050

Male to Female Ratio:
51:49

Admissions

Overall Acceptance Rate:
25%

Early Decision Acceptance Rate:
33%

Regular Acceptance Rate:
24%

Total Applicants:
15,761

Total Acceptances:
3,861

Freshman Enrollment:
1642

Yield (percentage of admitted students who actually enroll):
43%

Early Decision Available?
Yes

Early Action Available?
No

Total Early Decision Applicants: 1581

Total Early Decision Acceptances:
506

Early Decision One Deadline:
November 1

Early Decision One Notification:
December 15

Early Decision Reply-by Date:
January 2

Regular Decision Deadline:
January 2 (December 14 for an alumni interview)

Regular Decision Notification:
early April

Must Reply-By Date:
May 1

Regular Decision Notification:
April 15

Must Reply-By Date:
May 1

Common Application Accepted?
Yes

Supplemental Forms?
All students using the Common Application must file Duke's supplement for the application to be complete. A copy of the supplement is included with the Duke application or can be downloaded at http://www.duke.edu/web/ug-admissions/apply.htm

Duke Online Application Form:
www.duke.edu/web/ug-admissions/onlineapp.htm

Common Application Website:
www.commonapp.org

Admissions Phone:
(919) 684-3214

Admissions Website:
www.admissions.duke.edu

SAT I or ACT Required?
Both accepted

SAT I Range (25th – 75th Percentile):
1330 – 1520

SAT I Verbal Range (25th – 75th Percentile):
660 – 750

SAT I Math Range (25th – 75th Percentile):
670 – 770

Top 10% of High School Class:
88%

Application Fee:
$70

Financial Information

Tuition:
$30,720

Room and Board:
$8,525

Books and Supplies:
$940

Average Freshman need-based loan:
$3,613

Average Freshman need-based grant:
$22,831

Students Who Applied For Financial Aid:
44%

Students Who Applied For Financial Aid and Received It:
40%

Financial Aid Forms Deadline:
Feb 1

Financial Aid Phone:
(919) 684-6225

Financial Aid Website:
http://dukefinancialaid.duke.edu/

Academics

The Lowdown On...
Academics

Degrees Awarded:
Bachelor's
Master's
Doctoral Certificate
Post Bachelor's Certificate
First Professional

Most Popular Areas of Study:
18% economics
9% public policy analysis
8% biology
8% psychology
7% political science and government

Undergraduate Schools:

- Trinity College of Arts & Sciences
- Pratt School of Engineering
- Fuqua School of Business
- School of Nursing

Tenure/Tenure track Faculty:
1,498

Other Faculty:
866

Faculty with Terminal Degree:
93%

Student-to-Faculty Ratio:
9:1

Average Course Load:
12-15 credits (4-5 classes)

Special Degree Options:
Program II. Unlike Program I, which is the basic Trinity program, this is more of a create-your-own major. More information about this can be found at www.aas.duke.edu/trinity/program2/

AP Test Score Requirements:
Possible credit for scores of 4 or 5

IB Test Score Requirements:
Possible credit for scores of 6 or 7

For more information on AP and IB credit, try
www.duke.edu/web/ug-admissions/general/ap.htm

Sample Academic Clubs:

American Society of Civil Engineers (ASCE):
www.duke.edu/web/ASCE/

Association for Computing Machinery (ACM):
www.duke.edu/web/ACM/

Biology Majors Union: www.duke.edu/web/biomajors/

Biomedical Engineering Society (BMES):
www.duke.edu/web/bmes/

Cultural Anthropology Majors Union (CAMU):
www.duke.edu/web/camu/

CHANCE tutoring program: www.duke.edu/web/chance/

Duke Mock Trial: www.duke.edu/web/mocktrial/Mock.htm/

Duke Math Union: www.math.duke.edu/dumu/

National Society of Black Engineers: www.duke.edu/web/NSBE/

Psychology Majors' Union:
www.psych.duke.edu/ugrad/ugmajorsunion.html

PreMed Society: www.duke.edu/web/premed/

* For a complete list of Duke Clubs, and Organizations, visit www.duke.edu/org/org.html

Did You Know?

- The **Vice Provost for Interdisciplinary Studies** works with faculty members and administrators across the university to support interdisciplinary research, collaboration and instruction on Duke's Strategic Plan: "Building on Excellence".

Best Places to Study:
- Your room
- Lilly Library (East Campus)
- A comfy corner in the Bryan Center
- The Sanford Building
- Perkins Library (West Campus)
- East or West Campus Quad

Students Speak Out On...
Academics

> "In contrast to the horror stories I heard before getting to college, my teachers have all seemed genuinely interested in teaching undergrads."

Q "Many of them have their own research going on the side, but I don't sense that it detracts from the quality of their classes. **They tend to have their own little idiosyncrasies** that remind you they're real people. I'd have to say I've enjoyed most of my classes."

Q "When I was at Duke, **I thought the teachers sucked.** In retrospect, they weren't that bad, but that's how I felt when I was there."

Q "The professors are for the most part, amazing. **They know their subjects inside and out**, but better yet, are willing to help you understand (piece by piece) what they know. The classes don't just skim over things, but rather make you go in depth and have you learn things that you just wouldn't learn in a standard lecture."

Q "The teachers here are basically **Southerners to the core.** They aren't the most exciting teachers in the world, but they're okay."

Q "I found the professors to be **very down-to-earth** and always willing to help. They were all very accessible and seemed willing and able to do whatever it took in order for their students to succeed. I think that's a tribute to the professors themselves . . . they have ways of making the material interesting."

Q "The faculty at Duke is **a mixed bag**. I've had great professors and some that were really horrible. I guess it depends on your major, because most of the liberal arts people I know are happy with their teachers. I'm an economics and computer science major, and, with two exceptions, all my professors have sucked royally."

Q "The professors at Duke are fantastic. **Their lectures are engaging,** and I have gotten to know most of my professors on a personal basis. Most of the courses I take are in topics that interest me, so the classes are almost always interesting."

Q "In general, **the teachers are awesome!** They're passionate about their subjects and they get you excited about learning too. Also, I was really amazed at how available and willing to help most of them were; just ask, and they're glad to answer questions or meet with you outside of class."

Q "I had been warned that college professors were a little on the intimidating side, so I stayed clear of them in my first semester. After getting my grades, I realized **I had to speak up if I wanted to do better.** I was encouraged to come to office hours and lunches or to just e-mail my professors. Even if you're struggling in a class, you can do better if you show the professor you want to do well by just talking with them."

Q "Teachers at Duke are both **great and personable.** I worked for two professors and got really close to them throughout my college career. At the same time though, you have to take the initiative because you could easily get overlooked. The classes are small depending on your major (except for your intro classes), so you can easily form relationships with your professors"

Q "The professors know what they're doing and **genuinely care about their jobs.** They will teach you to the best of their abilities and encourage deep thinking among all their students. Your first-year writing and seminar classes will help with these skills."

Q "Well, just as everywhere, **the quality of teaching varies.** There are some incredibly wonderful professors and some grad students who really shouldn't be teaching classes just yet. It's best to ask an upperclassman. They'll know who's phenomenal and who's abominable."

Q "Often, the teachers here are great. Duke has an open-door policy so **you can contact the professors at any time.** At the law school, my professors were always available the night before an exam to answer questions. They often gave us their private phone numbers as well."

Q "Professors at Duke are all highly qualified, and **most are distinguished in their field.** In my first year of classes, my professors included a renowned fiction writer, a Nobel prize laureate, a member of Jimmy Carter's presidential cabinet, and a former military commander."

Q "The teachers at Duke are **typical college professors.** Most of them have a uniqueness that makes their class more interesting, and they really lecture too. But they do their job, and they do it well. The academic programs are notoriously excellent, and if you graduate from your courses, you should be set on a nicely paved career path."

The College Prowler Take On...
Academics

Students at Duke seem to have found the academic experience, thanks in large part due to their teachers, pretty satisfying on the whole. This is not to say that everything about Duke Academics is peachy; some of the math and science professors certainly sound like they could liven up a little. There is also the age-old problem of distinguished faculty who are there for the research facilities and not much else. However, researching professors can be a remarkable asset if they choose to keep students involved—which many are willing, able, and even excited to do. Even lecture classes need not be survival-only. Many lecturers take special care to get to know students one-on-one, and lectures will almost always have a lab or a discussion group taught by student TA's so students get more personal attention.

All Duke professors are well-educated and established in their field, and most students will tell you that the professors here do their best to relay their knowledge to the students in a way that is easily comprehensible, yet challenging at the same time. Faculty members are excited about their subjects and, more importantly, about teaching what they know to their students. Duke's professors play a vital role in the quality and success of its academics.

The College Prowler™ Grade on
Academics: A

A high Academics grade generally indicates that Professors are knowledgeable, accessible, and genuinely interested in their students' welfare. Other determining factors include class size, how well professors communicate, and whether or not classes are engaging.

Local Atmosphere

The Lowdown On...
Local Atmosphere

Region:
Southeast

City, State:
Durham, NC

Setting:
Suburban

Distance from the Beach:
3 hours

Closet Shopping Malls:
Southpoint Mall
6910 Fayetteville Rd
Durham, NC 27713
At I-40 Exit 276
Phone: (919) 572-8808

Northgate Mall
1058 West Club Blvd.
Durham, NC
At I-85 Exit 176A
Phone: (919) 286-4400
www.ngatemall.com/

Brightleaf Square
905 W. Main Street Suite 19 E.
Durham, NC
Phone: (919) 682-9229
www.brightleaf.citysearch.com/

Closest Movie Theatres:

Southpoint Cinemas
8030 Renaissance Parkway
The Streets of Southpoint
Durham, NC 27713
Phone: (919) 226-2000
www.movies.raleighlist.org/
Southpoint-Cinemas.htm

Carmike Wynnsong
1800 Martin Luther King Boulevard
Durham, NC 27717
(919) 489-9505
www.movies.raleighlist.org/
Carmike-Wynnsong.htm

Major Sports Teams:

Durham Bulls
(Minor League Baseball)

Carolina Courage
(Women's Soccer)

City Websites:

triangle.citysearch.com/
www.durham-nc.com

Did You Know?
5 Fun Facts About Durham

1. Durham is not named for its sister city, Durham, England, but rather for Dr. Bartlett Durham, who donated the four acres of land to **build a railroad station** around which the city developed.
2. Durham has several interesting **sister cities:** Toyama City, Japan; Kostroma, Russia; Arusha, Tanzania; and the afore mentioned Durham, England.
3. Durham used to be known as the "Bull City," but is now known as the **"City of Medicine,"** and is part of the Research Triangle.
4. The Triangle Area (Raleigh, Durham, Chapel Hill, and the surrounding cities) has one of the **highest concentrations of Ph.D.'s** in the world.
5. North Carolina was the site of man's **first mechanical flight** by the Wright Brothers. This event is commemorated on North Carolina's license plates, which read "First in Flight."

Famous People from Durham:

John H. Franklin - Historian & Presidential Medal of Freedom winner

Julian Abele - architect of Duke Chapel

Rev. Douglas Moore -pioneer of sit-ins in the Civil Rights Movement

Floyd McKissick, Sr. - civil rights leader & father of a Congressman

Dr Charles Johnson - president of the National Medical Association

Shirley Caesar - gospel vocalist

Clyde McPhatter - R&B vocalist for the Drifters

Neena Freelon - jazz vocalist

Coach John McClendon - basketball strategist still emulated today

→

Sam Jones - 1st African American drafted by NBA in the first round

Ernie Barnes – world-renown artist

Blind Boy Fuller - Piedmont Blues vocalist

Grady Tate - renowned jazz drummer

Branford Marsalis - Grammy-winning saxophonist and film score composer

Local Slang
If you're Southern you'll know it. If you're not, don't try it.

Students Speak Out On...
Local Atmosphere

> "Durham is flanked by Chapel Hill and Raleigh, the state capital. These areas are associated with UNC Chapel Hill and NC State, respectively."

Q "These universities represent great opportunities for off-campus fun. Duke's off-campus houses border a shady area of Durham called Walltown, basically an indigent, poverty-stricken neighborhood with all sorts of problems. **Walltown is not necessarily a slum,** but neither is it a wholesome place to live."

Q "**Durham is one big bore.** However, Chapel Hill is nice because it's a town built around a large university. Duke makes its own social scene since Durham doesn't provide one. There are at least six other colleges in the area."

Q "There are two colleges near Durham. One is fifteen minutes away in Chapel Hill (UNC), and the other is twenty minutes away in Raleigh (NC State). Durham has the Durham Bulls baseball team, the Carolina Hurricanes play nearby, and all of the college basketball teams in the area are stellar, so sports are huge. There's also a cool museum in Raleigh. **There's plenty to do in and around campus.**"

Q "**UNC Chapel Hill is a bus ride away.** If you have a car or friends to go out with, then you're set."

Q "**Durham is not a great city.** I tell people that Duke is not in Durham. Durham surrounds the campus, but the campus is very separate from the city. Ten minutes away is UNC-Chapel Hill, our main rival. Chapel Hill is much more of a college town than Durham. My advice is to always stay on campus."

Q "Duke and Durham are almost two completely separate worlds. **Durham is a rather small city,** and it isn't a typical college town. Don't expect to find the same culture or entertainment options you'd see in New York or Boston. Wandering into the wrong sections of town will leave you in a high-crime low-income area. I tend to spend most of my time on campus unless I'm headed out for dinner and a movie."

Q "**Durham is a friendly Southern city with the amenities of big-city living.** Some good places to go are Ninth Street (for shopping and dining), the new mall, and the streets at Southpoint. Seven miles west of Durham is Chapel Hill, which is more of a college town and has more things to do on Franklin Street."

Q "The atmosphere is really cool, and diverse. Restaurants are great; there's a lot to do. **You could have an awesome social life** without ever leaving campus."

Q "I really don't get out much in Durham. However **Chapel Hill, home of UNC, is a vibrant, exciting city.** There are lots of restaurants in both cities—always something for everyone. I would stay away from downtown Durham at night and Fayetteville Road in general. Stuff to visit would have to include the Duke Gardens, the Museum of Life and Science for the kids (or immature biologists), and historic Raleigh, about 40 minutes away."

Q "Sadly, **Durham and Duke don't have the best ties.** Some of this might be due to the self-contained nature of [the] Duke campus. There is, however, Ninth Street, which offers many restaurants and shops. Durham has two malls in the vicinity; the challenge is transportation. Chapel Hill is also in the area, and happens to be a much better college town than Durham (we can thank UNC for that, and only that)."

Q "Durham is an **old tobacco town that had its day in the sun a while ago.** Luckily, the area as a whole (the Triangle) has grown immensely and areas around Durham (Chapel Hill, Raleigh, and the in-betweens) are getting some nice and exciting attractions. My favorite spot is actually Franklin Street in Chapel Hill."

Q "Most Duke students, me included, don't tend to spend a lot of time in Durham. There's a lot to do on campus, so I don't know too much about what Durham is really like. I don't recommend walking around off-campus after dark because **Durham has a fairly high crime rate**, but there are things to do within driving distance. Off-campus, there are lots of restaurants, The Streets at Southpoint mall, and the Durham Bulls."

The College Prowler Take On...
Local Atmosphere

As much as the students love Duke, there are some shortcomings that simply cannot be overlooked. The atmosphere or lack thereof, is at the top of the list. At the beginning of freshman year, Student Life Officials herd all the first year students into the commons room and do their best to scare everyone out of ever wandering around Durham alone. While East Campus is not situated near the nicest part of Durham, there are a few nice, quiet little residential areas around East Campus as well as some adequate shopping centers and restaurants within driving distance. Ninth Street, just off of East Campus (within short walking distance), is where most students choose to go for off-campus restaurants and some shops. West Campus is much more isolated from Durham, so students won't really sense the Durham atmosphere unless they go looking for it.

If you're looking for a college town, Chapel Hill lives up to that description quite nicely, and is no more than twenty minutes away. Duke and UNC provide a free bus back and forth every day, which many students take advantage of. The bus usually runs until about 11 p.m., but stops at 5 p.m. on Saturdays. For the most part though, Duke's campus is quite self-contained, and many students never feel the need to leave. Other than Ninth Street, Durham has little in the way of atmosphere to offer students.

C

The College Prowler™ Grade on Local Atmosphere: C

A high Local Atmosphere grade indicates that the area surrounding campus is safe and scenic. Other factors include nearby attractions, proximity to other schools, and the town's attitude toward students

Safety & Security

The Lowdown On...
Safety & Security

Number of Duke University Police:
51 sworn police officers
51 non-sworn security officers

Phone:
(919) 684-2444 (non-emergency)

Duke Police Website:
www.duke.edu/web/police/

DUPD-CP provides the following services:
Educational programs
Facility surveys
Security system design and upgrade recommendations
Crime tracking & analysis

Safety Services:
Card-only access to dorms
Same-sex keyed bathrooms
Safe Rides
Blue light phones
Safety lighting
Self-defense classes

Services Available through the Student Health Center:

Allergy clinic
Cold/flu/allergy self-help tables
Gynecological services
Health education
Health exams
HIV counseling and testing
Laboratory
Medical care
Nutritional counseling
Pharmacy
Physical therapy
Substance abuse education
Travel/immunization clinic
X-rays

Duke Health Center Hours:

By Appointment Monday-Friday 8:30 a.m.-5:30 p.m.
Phone: (919) 681-9355

Healthy Devil Wellness and Fitness Assessment Center

Hours: By appointment only
Phone: (919) 684-5610

East Campus Wellness Clinic

Hours: Walk-in, Monday-Friday 8 a.m.-4:30 p.m.
Phone: (919) 613-1111

Student Health Physical Therapy

Hours: Walk-in, Monday-Friday 2 p.m.-4:30 p.m.
Phone: (919) 684-6480

More info on the Health Center can be found at:
www.healthydevil.studentaffairs.duke.edu

Students Speak Out On...
Safety & Security

"I got my car stolen sophomore year, but that's because I was an idiot. The guy got arrested before I even knew the car was stolen. If you're on campus, you'll feel completely safe. The ghetto lingers, but it's not that bad."

Q "I've never really felt unsafe on campus. The university has its own campus police, and there are phones scattered across campus to call for help if you need it. You'll need a student ID in order to enter any of the dorms. Most other buildings require ID on nights and weekends. Unlike some schools, **officers don't regularly guard campus or building entrances.** We had a few sexual assault reports last year, but I don't know if it's higher than average or not."

Q "As far as security goes, it seems that **the campus police are more concerned with parking violations than anything else** (obviously the most important part of police work). You're basically safe on campus, but the surrounding area isn't a sure bet (I'm used to it, so it doesn't bother me). I've heard people complain about homeless people begging for money and the usual city nuisances."

Q "There is good safety in the main areas, and response time from police or 911 is very good. However, due in part to the fact that Duke is a very wooded campus, **security outside the main areas is few and far between.** Lack of lighting is a major problem that needs improvement."

Q "**There are numerous problems with Duke Gardens at night** (you'd walk through this area to cross from west campus to central campus). Two of my friends got robbed at gunpoint twice doing just that. More than a little caution is necessary."

Q "I've never had a problem with feeling safe on campus. Although **Durham has a bad reputation for safety,** Duke has their own police force on campus, and I know they patrol frequently. I'd say that if someone uses common sense, he or she should generally be safe."

Q "**Cars get broken into left and right,** so keep that in mind if you're going to bring one. One of my friends had his stereo stolen, and his car wasn't exactly a thief's dream."

Q "Security has beefed up a lot lately, but there were some problems last year. **One student was attacked in a dorm bathroom**, and another was attacked in a library bathroom. Cars are sometimes broken into, and there have been a few muggings at night, when students have been walking alone. So just use common sense and you should be safe."

Q "Security has gotten a lot better on campus with **guards patrolling the campus more at night.** However, parking lots and other places around campus can be extremely scary. Luckily, Duke offers services like SafeRides that you can call twenty-four hours a day."

Q "There is very tight security, but **some areas still feel dangerous**—especially the main library late at night, because you can't see who's around you in the stacks. Duke Police are on bikes throughout campus and patrol parking lots everywhere."

Q "Last year, there were **some issues with robberies** on campus (mostly in the gardens very late at night) but security patrols were stepped up, and if you stay on the lighted paths you should be fine."

Q "I personally feel pretty safe here. The campus police actually picked me up once for being a 'female walking alone' between campuses at night (yeah, that was dumb). We do, of course, have the odd incident, but each time, there has been a quick response from the administration. For example, a man hid in one of the girls' bathrooms, and now **bathrooms must be opened with a room key.**"

Q "Students at Duke live in what is essentially a closed environment. Access to the campus is restricted both geographically and legally. **Isolated incidents of non-violent crime are occasional** on campus, but not too prevalent."

Q "Security on campus is about average for any college campus. Most of the students are fairly well behaved, and there really haven't been any incidents to speak of. **You would be perfectly safe on campus**, I have no doubt."

Q "Security is good on campus, but a girl can't walk around by herself at night because **the east campus area isn't the best.** There are lots of emergency phones and police around though, so I never feel unsafe as long as I'm not alone."

Q "Security and safety could definitely be improved on campus. **Many walkways and parking lots are poorly lit** at night. The dorms feel pretty secure, though, as card access is required for entry."

The College Prowler Take On...
Safety & Security

Most Duke students feel pretty secure on campus, and Duke has worked hard to provide students with the utmost safety and comfort. Duke has implemented, and expanded upon, many safety measures that are becoming standard on many college campuses, like carded entry to dorms and other facilities. Students are also briefed on methods for getting anyone out of the dorm who they don't think should be there. The bathrooms are also locked and, as of last year, the bathroom keys will open only the same-sex bathroom in your dorm as opposed to the old keys that would open any bathroom on any floor (sorry boys!). Campus always seems to have people milling about, but if you're walking through Edens or Central late at night, it might be best to bring along a friend - preferably a tall, muscular one. Duke likes to keep students updated on safety and security measures. However, Duke is not in a very attractive area of Durham, and walking alone off campus is extremely unwise, and there are occasionally thefts and robberies that occur on campus.

Duke tries hard to keep its students safe. However, the old real-estate maxim ("location, location, location") should serve to remind us that Duke has some inherent problems simply because of the instability of the surrounding area. Fortunately, very few Duke students feel like they have to stay holed up in their rooms at night staring out the windows at the lurking shadows below. The best advice has already been given a number of times: "Use your brain."

C

The College Prowler™ Grade on

A high grade in Safety & Security means that students generally feel safe, campus police are visible, blue light phones and escort services are readily available, and safety precautions are not overly necessary.

Computers

The Lowdown On...
Computers

High-Speed Network?
Yes, LAN network. Students provide their own cables

Wireless Network?
Yes, users must register but use is free and the network works almost everywhere on campus

Downloadable Software:
Antivirus Software
Math/ Statistical Software
Utilities
Security, SSH/SFTP and Firewalls
Internet Software
X-Windows
Office Suites

Did You Know?

- Computer Labs:
www.oit.duke.edu/ats/labs/
- West Campus: 12
- East Campus: 6
- Central campus: 1
- Numbers of Computers: 340
- Platforms: Windows, Macintosh, Unix, Linux
- Number of Labs: West Campus: 12, East Campus: 6
Central campus: 1

24-Hour Labs:

• **All labs are open twenty-four hours a day** while classes are in session except Lilly, which is open only during library hours. Some labs (Brown, Carr, Gilbert-Addoms, Lilly, Hudson, and Old Chem) may be reserved for classes at some times. Many labs offer onsite lab support which is only available from 6 p.m. to 10 p.m. Sunday through Thursday

Charge to Print?
No

Students Speak Out On...
Computers

> "The Duke Intranet is amazing—one of the most extensive, best-run, and fastest I have used. That said, PC and Mac computer labs are generally crowded (Unix labs are often empty), so I would highly recommend bringing a computer."

Q "Most **students prefer laptops,** but guard it carefully—at least one laptop is reported stolen every week."

Q "The computer network is **incredibly fast**—I miss it when I'm at home! The computer labs aren't generally very crowded, but I recommend bringing a computer because the labs don't always have the best computers in the world. They aren't bad, but just about any new computer will be better. Plus, it's a whole lot more convenient to have a computer right there in the dorm."

Q "The computer **labs aren't too bad.** There are a decent amount of them, so you can usually find someplace to work. I'd still recommend that you bring your own computer, if it's not a problem. You'll find things are easier that way, and you're going to want easy Internet access."

Q "During finals and the end of the semester the computer labs will get filled up, but it's **far better to bring your own computer.** Laptops are usually the most convenient and there are internet plugs around campus and wireless internet."

Q "**Computer clusters are great,** but bring your own if you can. It's easier."

Q "Bringing your own computer is nice, but the computer labs on East campus (where you will be living freshman year) have adequate space. Additionally, **you can store up to 70 MB in your personal file system** on the network."

Q "The computer network was great; **I miss the fast connection.** Computer labs can be pretty full at different times of the day, but if you don't mind using a Mac, you can get on before too long."

Q "**Why are you even thinking about not bringing a computer?** Computer labs are fairly easy to get to, open 24/7, and usually have open machines, but the convenience of having your own computer will outweigh the cost every time. There aren't any monthly download or bandwidth limits that I know of."

Q "Your own computer will provide comfort, and if you have the resources by all means bring one. However, **the computer labs are always accessible** (you might have a very short wait during 'peak' times like exams), are in convenient places, and are conducive to working."

Q "It's rather fast; you can pull a movie off the network in maybe three minutes. Duke provides software for e-mail, file transfer, Unix shell, and such, so **you can do everything on your own computer.** Some classes also have web assignments or tests that you probably won't want to do in a computer cluster."

Q "Most students have their own computer or notebook so that they don't have to use the university's computers. As a consequence, **the labs aren't too crowded.** There are lots of possibilities to log into the network. Bringing your own computer is just an added burden."

Q "I think that bringing your own computer is essential to academic life at Duke, but **I do know a few students who do well without one.** The network is fast and trouble free, and typically virus and worm free. Computer labs are never filled to capacity and are populated with different types of computers for different applications such as Macs and PCs for student work, and Sun Unix workstations for engineering and computer science students."

Q **"Computer labs are crowded only around exams.**
Many classes, however, use a lot of Internet applications, so a personal computer is almost a necessity. I'd bring a desktop over a laptop; portability might only be a problem for freshmen and off-campus students."

The College Prowler Take On...
Computers

Duke's network seldom fails to make all the internet junkies across campus quiver with delight. It's fast, easily acessible, and well-maintained. As for computers labs, some (like Perkins) almost always require a short wait, but most have plenty of open computers to offer. During midterms and finals, of course, when people are desperately writing papers, it's much harder to find an available computer. This serves mostly to encourage the common conception that although you can function without a computer, it's much nicer to have one. If you're going to bring a computer, and aren't a computer science major who needs two towers to take apart on those lonely Friday nights, so consider bringing a laptop. There is nothing as convenient as being able to carry around this revolutionary little piece of machinery and write, work, take notes, listen to music, and more wherever you go.

Students at Duke generally have few complaints about either the labs or the network. Labs can, of course, become crowded around finals, but you'd be hard pressed to find a University where that's not the case. You won't be rendered obsolete without your own personal computer, but in the event that you bring one, you will be able to take advantage of Duke's exceptional network capabilities.

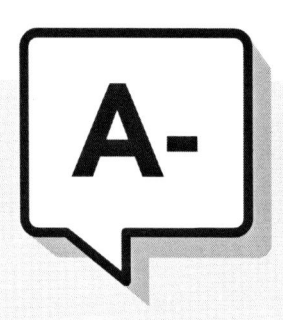

A-

The College Prowler™ Grade on

A high grade in Computers designates that computer labs are available, the computer network is easily accessible, and the campus' computing technology is up to date.

Facilities

The Lowdown On...
Facilities

Student Center:
Bryan Center ("the BC")

Athletic Center:
West Campus: Wilson Recreation Center, Intramural Building

East Campus: Brodie Recreation Center

Popular Places to Chill:
The main quads
Your dorm bench
Couches in the BC

Libraries:
Perkins (West Campus)
Lilly (East Campus)
Music Library (East Campus, Biddle Building)
Vesic Library for Engineering, Math, and Physics (Science Drive)
Biological and Environmental Sciences Library (Science Drive, Bio Sci Building)
Chemistry Library (Science Drive, Gross Chem Building)

Professional School Libraries: Ford Business Library, Divinity Library, Law School Library, Medical Center Library

What Is There to Do On Campus?

If you can find a DUI (Duke University Improv) performance, go to it! Duke's A Capella groups are abundant and awesome, and there are some exceptional dance groups as well. Local Colour, Duke's spoken word group, is also worth going to see. Plays are sometimes a mixed bag, but Broadway at Duke brings in some professional flair. Movies in the Griffith Film Theater are either cheap or free, and the theater shows some amazing films from time to time.

Movie Theatre on Campus?
Yes, Griffith Film Theater in the BC

Bowling on Campus?
No

Billiards on Campus?
Yes, one table in the BC lounge, two more in the WEL

Bar on Campus?
No

Coffeehouse on Campus?
Yes

Trinity Café:
East Campus Union Building. This past year Trinity Café offered "Trinity nights," having student bands come in and perform on Friday nights. This coming year you may find karaoke and poetry readings here as well.

The Perk:
West Campus, Floor two of Perkins, next to the Gothic Reading room.

Blue Devil Beanery:
The WEL, in McClendon tower. The only on-campus coffeehouse to offer Starbucks coffee.

Students Speak Out On...
Facilities

> "The recreation center is excellent, the computer labs are above average (they just renovated a couple of them), and the student center is okay, but it's mostly just a place to put the on-campus restaurants. The school movie theatre is a little lacking, as far as quality is concerned."

Q "**I'm always impressed with the facilities** at Duke. They are always building something new. The campus is always under construction. Everything is pretty upscale."

Q "**The gym on West Campus is extremely nice.** They have enough treadmills and elliptical machines to keep the cardio folks happy, and the weight room is positively superb. Free weights, machines, whatever your pleasure is–it's available and in good condition. Throw in a few racquetball courts, basketball courts, a pool, and a juice bar, and you've got a very high quality fitness center."

Q "**Wilson is a much nicer gym than Brodie**; but for us non-athletic nerds, [Brodie] is better suited to try to play basketball."

Q "The exterior of practically **every building at Duke is breathtaking;** old and Gothic or Georgian, new and innovative, exciting even. The inside sometimes doesn't evoke the same pleasant adjectives, particularly in the older buildings. The buildings on east campus are nice, but the ones on west campus are somewhat dark and cramped. All of the newer buildings I have seen are great, and the athletic buildings are made in the mode of shrines and palaces for kings."

Q "Every facility is at a different level of quality. As expected, **the newer and recently renovated buildings are the nicest**, while the older buildings with their grungy basements are the worst. The dining facilities are all excellent. The student center is great, but difficult to navigate and due for renovation."

Q **"All the facilities here are top-notch**. The gym on the East Campus is good, the gym on the West Campus is excellent. Lots of machines and free weights are always available, and we have an indoor pool and lots of tennis and basketball courts both indoors and out."

Q "Most of the facilities are really nice. There are athletic centers on both East and West campuses, and of course Cameron Indoor Stadium is really neat (although not as big as it looks on TV). The Bryan Center is an adequate place to hang out, but I think **the dorm commons rooms are a lot more convenient."**

Q "Duke facilities are excellent. **They are convenient**, up-to-date, clean, and provide a very enjoyable environment. I'd rank Duke facilities among the best in the country."

Q "**Athletic facilities are very good here.** There's Brodie Rec Center on East and Wilson on West. You can go to either—I haven't been to Wilson yet, but Brodie has a lot of exercise machines, a nice weight room, and lots of kickboxing/aerobics classes. I've heard Wilson has even more of everything."

Q "Athletic facilities are awesome here, especially on West Campus. There are computers everywhere, including the two main libraries. **I'm a big fan of the student center** as well. I'd live there if they'd let me!"

Q "The facilities better be nice; **they reflect the amount of funding that goes into them.** The facilities are hardly ever lacking. Our tuition money does not get wasted."

The College Prowler Take On...
Facilities

Duke is a beautiful campus, and the buildings are well-kept. The original Gothic buildings on Main West quad and the Georgian buildings on Main East are simply stunning. Newer buildings receive mixed reviews regarding beauty—The Sanford Institute of Public Policy, for example, is elegant and modern while the Gross Chemistry building just around the corner is (perhaps because of its name) generally considered one of the uglier buildings on campus. The athletic centers are really quite pleasant and well-kept (especially Wilson; Brodie is serviceable but not spectacular). The Bryan Student Center tends to draw some very mixed reviews. Although it is reasonably central to West Campus and brings together restaurants, recreation, and administration just as a student center ought, the extensive use of concrete pillars and walls as interior decorating choices garners some complaints. A plan, scheduled for the summer of 2004, to overhaul the BC walkway and replace it with a huge concrete plaza has been reconsidered and, if it begins at all, wouldn't start till the summer of 2005. Lilly Library on East Campus is quite beautiful, but Perkins on East suffers from some 70's décor and the curse of stacks, which are as intimidating as they are in any other university. Fortunately the libraries make up for any lack of outer beauty with their extensive collections.

Despite the griping and minor complaints, Duke has some pretty darn nice facilities. This is not to say that all of the buildings on campus are spacious and immaculate—but it should be made clear that Duke, like so many of its students, is physically beautiful and well-groomed.

A-

The College Prowler™ Grade on
Facilities: A-

A high Facilities grade indicates that the campus is aesthetically pleasing and well maintained, facilities are state-of-the-art, and libraries are exceptional. Other determining factors include the quality of both athletic and student centers and an abundance of things to do on campus.

Campus Dining

The Lowdown On...
Campus Dining

Freshman Meal Plan Requirement?
Yes

Meal Plan Average Cost: Freshman Year:
$1,880-$2,015

Upper-Class Dining Plan:
$1,315-$2,030

Duke University Dining
Website: auxweb.duke.edu/Dining/

Casual Dining:
Alpine Atrium
Location: The BC, lower level
Favorites: Thai Chicken Wrap

Alpine Bagels and Brews
Location: West Union Building
Favorites: Banana Walnut with Honey Cinnamon Butter

Armadillo Grill
Location: The BC, Middle level
Favorites: guacamole tacos

The Blue Devil Beanery
Location: The WEL, McClendon Tower
Food: coffee shop fare

The Blue Express
Location: Levine Science Research Center
Favorites: gyros, every Tuesday

Cambridge Inn and Chick-fil-A
Location: West Union, first floor
Favorites: Cosmic Cantina bean-and-cheese burrito

Freeman Center for Jewish Life
Location: corner of Swift and Alexander
Favorites: Rosemary Chicken

Grace's Café
Location: Trent
Favorites : the fresh fruit and the Mongolian Beef plate

The Loop
Location: West Union Building)
Favorites:Loop N' Cheddar w/a Chocolate Malt, or Tomato Bisque

The Marketplace
Location: East Campus, Union Building
Favorites: hamburgers and fries

McDonald's
Location: The BC, middle level

Pauly Dogs
Location: West Union patio
Favorites: the hot dogs

Quenchers
Location: Wilson Recreation Center
Favorites: excellent smoothies

Rick's Diner
Location: The WEL, McClendon Tower
Favorites: Caesar Salad with Chicken

Subway & Breyer's
Location: West Union Building

Trinity Café
Location: East Campus Union
Food: coffee shop fare

On-campus table-service restaurants on points:

The Blue Bistro in the Oak Room
Location:West Union
Favorites: Grilled Salmon

The Fairview Restaurant
Location: Washington Duke Inn and Golf Club
Favorites: Rack of Lamb
Reservations Suggested.
(919) 493-6699

Off-Campus Places to Use Your Meal Plan:

Off-Campus restaurants will only deliver on points. If you go to the restaurant, you will need to pay in cash.

Cattleman's Grill
(919) 382-3292
Delivery: Monday-Friday: 6 p.m.-11 p.m.; Saturday and Sunday: 1 p.m.-11 p.m.

Domino's Pizza
(919) 682-3030
Delivery: 10:30 a.m.-3 a.m.

Francesca's Italian Grill
(919) 286-4242
Delivery: Monday-Friday: 6 p.m.-11 p.m.; Saturday-Sunday: 1 p.m.-11 p.m.

George's Garage
(919) 416-0842 or (919) 416-6631
Delivery: Monday-Friday: 6 p.m.-10 p.m.; Saturday-Sunday: 5:30 p.m.-10 p.m.

Grace's Café
(919) 660-3966
Delivery: Sunday-Friday: 10 a.m.-9 p.m.

Jimmy John's
(919) 286-5383
Delivery Hours: TBA

La Fonte Restaurant
(919) 383-9001
Delivery: Monday-Friday 7 p.m.-Midnight; Saturday-Sunday: 1 p.m.-Midnight

Papa John's Pizza
(919) 682-7272
Delivery: Monday-Friday: 7 p.m.-2 a.m.; Saturday-Sunday: 1 p.m.-3 a.m.

Satisfaction Restaurant
(919) 683-3853
Delivery: Monday-Saturday: 5 p.m.-10 p.m.

Subs, Etc. & TCBY
(919) 309-4856
Delivery: Monday-Thursday: 7 p.m.-10 p.m.; Friday: 7 p.m.-11 p.m.; Saturday: 1 p.m.-11 p.m.; Sunday: 1 p.m.-9 p.m.

Torero's
(919) 286-0404
Delivery: 6 p.m.-1:30 a.m.

Wild Bull's Pizza
(919) 286-0590
Delivery: Monday-Thursday: 7 p.m.-2:30 a.m.; Friday: 7 p.m.-4 a.m.; Saturday: 5 p.m.-4 a.m.; Sunday: 5 p.m.-1 a.m.

Did You Know?

- All on-campus restaurants and cafeterias accept **food points ($1=1 point)**. Duke has a system that off-campus restaurants also deliver food paid for on points. This means pizza, steaks, subs, Chinese, Middle Eastern, Italian, Mexican, etc. are all delivered to your door without you having to dish up extra dough.

24-Hour On-Campus Eating?
Rick's Diner

Student Favorites:
The Loop, The Great Hall, Armadillo Grill

Students Speak Out On...
Campus Dining

"Campus food tends to be decent, but eating in the dining halls all the time will bore your taste buds after a while. Subway is popular for lunch. The Loop serves up pretty good pizza and burgers, and the milkshakes are quite enjoyable too."

Q "If you're looking for greasy Mexican food, Armadillo Grill is the place to be. **It'll destroy your arteries,** but it's worth it. The more traditional dining halls are the Great Hall and the Marketplace. You'll have an all-you-can-eat meal plan at the Marketplace freshman year. Meals there are hit or miss. The fruit and the meat are a little shady, but the pasta is usually safe."

Q "For the most part, **I really like the food in the dining hall.** It definitely doesn't compare to home-cooked meals, but there seems to be lots of variety. And there is a nice variety of other eateries on campus, such as the Loop, Alpine, and Armadillo Grill."

Q "The food is pretty good, and I think **the meal plans cover almost all the places on campus.** The Great Hall is a cafeteria with pretty good food and lots of variety, and The Loop has good sandwiches and pizza. There is also a hot dog stand and a Breyer's ice cream shop. Eating at the hospital is always a good choice, as it is cheap and there are several places in the food court."

Q "I would give Dukes dining situation an 'A' compared to food options at other schools, but I'll admit **you get tired of it quickly.** Freshmen have a meal plan that offers all-you-can-eat from a dining hall called the Marketplace, but everyone is tired of it by the end of the year."

Q "The food on campus is good. **It's lacking in fruits and vegetables**, but there are a variety of restaurants and cafes on campus."

Q "Food is **excellent as a freshman and good as a senior.** They have a points system and partner with a lot of restaurants off-campus, so you get really good food through the delivery service."

Q "Though you will undoubtedly hear griping about the food from Aramark and jokes about Marketplace food, **Duke food is considered some of the best** among the universities in this nation. I don't know whether that's a testament to Duke or to how bad food is at every university."

Q "As a freshman, you will receive a first-year plan, which gives you 12 meals a week at the east campus Marketplace—they serve breakfast Monday-Friday, dinner Sunday-Thursday, and brunch Saturday and Sunday, all all-you-can-eat—along with a choice of three debit dining accounts, known as 'points.' The meals cannot be banked (carried over), and honestly, I don't see a reason to. **You'll eat enough.**"

Q "You can always add money to your points account in increments of $25. **The Marketplace is also open for lunch,** but not on an all-you-can-eat basis; it is charged to your points account. During lunch, you have your choice of deli-carved sandwiches, hamburgers, hot dogs, chicken sandwiches, and other delicacies. There are other locations on campus for food, such as Trinity Cafe, Armadillo Grill (Mexican food), Chik-fil-A, The Loop, and the Great Hall."

Q "**Food is not at its healthiest on campus.** Good spots are Grace's in Trent, the Marketplace on East, and Great Hall on West."

Q "Okay, well, by this point, I'm sure you know that all freshmen live on East Campus and must buy a meal plan at The Marketplace. I thought the food there was fine at the beginning of the year, and they made several improvements last semester. There are several bars with a different main course every night and some staples that are available every night (pizza, pasta with marinara sauce, sandwiches, and salads). **The Great Hall on West Campus works off of your points account,** so you can buy meals there, but I haven't done that very often."

Q "**As a freshman, you'll eat breakfast and dinner in the Market Place** over on east campus. On West Campus, we have a pizza and burger joint called The Loop, a Mexican place, McDonald's, a really good cafeteria, a couple of delis, and a restaurant called the Oak Room. There are also many places off-campus that will make deliveries on food points."

Q "The food on campus is **way better for upperclassmen than for freshmen!** Freshmen are required to buy a dining plan that includes twelve meals a week in the Marketplace, the dining hall on East Campus, and while the food there isn't bad, it gets really monotonous. However, for the other meals freshmen have the same options as everyone else. My favorites are the Loop, which serves gourmet pizzas and sandwiches, and Armadillo Grill, which serves Mexican food."

Q "Food on campus is quite good, and **you have several dinning halls.** In the student center, there is a McDonald's and a Mexican restaurant. At the different schools there are also cafeterias where you can eat during lunch time."

Q "**Freshmen at Duke are given two meals per day** at a diverse on-campus cafeteria called The Marketplace. Though the food is good, it gets old quickly. Fortunately, there is a plethora of other dining choices on campus that fit into students' meal plans—The Loop, The Oak Room, Armadillo Grill, etc."

Q "I'm a vegetarian, so my view is probably a bit different than most. Of course, you've probably heard of the freshmen meal plan, but in case you haven't—all freshmen have the same meal plan, which includes breakfast on Monday through Friday, dinner on Sunday through Thursday, and brunch on Saturday and Sunday. All of those meals must be eaten at the Marketplace, which is decent. Not good, but not bad either. **My favorite is Alpine Atrium,** which is a cafe over on West in the Bryan Center (the student union for upperclassmen)."

Q "The cafeteria food is decent, though **it gets old after awhile.** The quality seems to rejuvenate itself around family and alumni weekends. The campus offers a million options with points that are initially delicious, but, frankly, going to the same restaurants all the time is boring. I need more variety."

Q "I've seen the slop of other schools and in comparison ours is [definitely better]. **We can get steaks six days a week and seafood.** They definitely try hard to make sure we're well fed (just check out my freshmen and then sophomore fifteen). My favorite places to eat are The Loop and The Great Hall."

The College Prowler Take On...
Campus Dining

You'll hear plenty of complaints about the freshman meal plan, and many of them are justified. This meal plan requires freshmen to eat breakfast and dinner at the Marketplace every weekday (except Friday, when it's only breakfast) as well as brunch on Saturday and Sunday. On the one hand this is very convenient: you eat dinner with your friends every night and don't have to worry about paying for over-priced fast food. On the other hand, although the food is really not nearly as bad as everyone will tell you, it really wears on you after a while. West Campus, however, abounds with places to eat. Until you finally break down and beg for homemade food, West and Science Drive should be able to satisfy all your cravings, as well as creating a few.

Duke's food service is known to be among the best in the nation, but students will complain anyway. If you can't find something you like on campus, you can use points to order from off-campus. If you can't find something you like there, pack up and go home because you won't find better college food anywhere else.

B+

The College Prowler™ Grade on Campus Dining: B+

Our grade on Campus Dining addresses the quality of both school-owned dining halls and independent on campus restaurants as well as the price, availability, and variety of food available.

Off-Campus Dining

The Lowdown On...
Off-Campus Dining

Restaurant Prowler:
Popular Places to Eat!

Anotherthyme
Food: Eclectic & International, Vegetarian
Address: 109 N Gregson St
Phone: (919) 682-5225

Bahn's Cuisine
Food: Vietnamese and Chinese
Address: 750 Ninth Street
Phone: (919) 286-5073

Ben & Jerry's
Food: classic Ben & Jerry flavors
Address: 609 Broad Street
Phone: (919) 416-6128

Beverly's Diner
Food: homemade diner fare
Address: 1807 Markham Avenue
Phone: (919) 286-5789

Blue Corn Café
Food: Latin American
Address: 716-B Ninth Street
Phone: (919) 286-9600

Bruegger's Bagels
Food: Bagels & Bagel Sandwiches
Address: 626 Ninth Street
Phone: (919) 286-7897

Bullock's Bar B Cue
Food: Southern Cooking
Address: 3330 Quebec Dr.
Phone: (919) 383-3211

California Pizza Kitchen
Food: Pizza
Address: 6910 Fayetteville Rd
Phone: (919) 361-4200

Cattleman's
Food: American
Address: 3211 Hillsborough Road
Phone: (919) 382-3292

Champp's Americana
Food: American
Address: 8030 Renaissance Pkwy
Phone: (919) 361-3393

Chili's Grill and Bar
Food: Mexican
Address: 4600 Durham Chapel Hill Blvd
Phone: (919) 489-6699

Cinelli's Pizza
Food: Pizza & Italian
Address: 607 Broad St
Phone: (919)416-4554

Cosmic Cantina
Food: California-style Mexican food,
Address: 1920 Perry Street
(919) 286-1875

Domino's
Food: Pizza
Address: 1209 W. Main Street
Phone; (919) 682-3030

Elmo's Diner
Food: family-style diner
Address: 776 Ninth Street
Phone: (919) 416-3823

Francesca's Dessert Café
Food: Café atmosphere,
Address: 706-B Ninth Street
Phone: (919) 286-4242

George's Garage
Food: Mediterranean, Seafood bar
Address: 737 Ninth Street
Phone: (919) 286-4131
Price: $21 to $30

Honey's
Food: Southern & Soul
Address: 2700 Guess Rd.
Phone: (919) 477-2181

New York Pizza
Food: Brooklyn-style pizzas, etc.
Address: 742 Ninth Street
Phone: (919) 416-1777

International Delights
Food: Middle Eastern- best baklava
Address: 740 Ninth Street
Phone: (919) 286-2884

Jimmy John's Subs
Food: Gourmet sandwiches
Address: 738 Ninth Street
(919) 286-538

Kallisti
Food: Italian/American salads, pizza
Address: 748 Ninth Street
Phone: (919) 286-0404

The Lounge
Food: the bar of Cosmic Cantina
Address: 1920 Perry Street
Phone: (919) 286-7441

Magnolia Grill
Food: American (New and Regional)
Address: 1002 Ninth Street
Phone: (919) 286-3609

McDonald's Drug Store
Food: old-fashioned soda fountain
Address: 732 Ninth Street
Phone: (919) 286-1115

Owen's Broad Street Diner
Food: voted best diner
Address: 1802 W. Main Street
Phone: (919) 416-6102

Outback Steakhouse
Food: Steakhouse
Address: 3500 Mount Moriah Rd
Phone: (919) 493-2202

PieWorks
Food: pizza
Address: 607 Broad Street
Phone: (919) 286-0404

Red Lobster
Food: Seafood
 4416 Durham Chapel Hill Blvd
Phone: (919) 493-3566

Romano's Macaroni Grill
Food: Italian
 4020 Durham Chapel Hill Blvd
Phone: (919) 489-0313

Ruby Tuesday's
Food: American
Address: 1058 W Club Blvd
Phone: (919) 286-5100

Spartacus
Food: Greek
Address: 4139 Chapel Hill Blvd.
Phone: (919) 489-2848

Wild Bull's Pizza
Food: Italian & Pizza
Address: 609 Trent Dr.
Phone: (919) 286-0590

Best Pizza:
Wild Bull's

Best Chinese:
Banh's

Best Breakfast:
Elmo's

Best Wings:
Cattleman's

Best Healthy:
Cosmic Cantina, Eno's

Best Place to Take Your Parents:
Elmo's

24-Hour Eating:
Honey's

Closest Grocery Store

Wellspring Grocery, 621 Broad Street, (919) 286-2290

Whole Foods Market, 605 Broad St., (919) 286-0765

Students Speak Out On...
Off-Campus Dining

> "There are a lot of really good places to eat off-campus, although not many within walking distance. Within walking distance on Ninth Street, students can get pizza, bagels, sandwiches, or a variety of ethnic foods."

Q "Cosmic Cantina is right off of East Campus. Hungry at 3 a.m.? **Go there for burritos.** Ninth St. is also nearby, but most of the food there is more suited to a quick meal than a real dinner. The diner, Elmo's, has some good entrees. If you have a car (or a friend with a car), check out Champps and California Pizza Kitchen at Southpoint mall."

Q "There is a highway that runs around the perimeter of Durham, and **there are several good restaurants along it.** There is also a new mall with some good places, and a lot of good places to eat in Chapel Hill."

Q "**Cosmic Cantina is the main off-campus spot;** it's always full of Duke students on weekends, and they stay open until four in the morning. It's like the after-after-party spot. People go to grab food together around two or three in the morning on Saturday nights. There are a lot of other places to eat off campus that are very close by, but because of the Duke student meal plan, people don't eat off-campus very much."

Q "**Off-campus restaurants are awesome.** The high-end places include PariZades, Magnolia Grill, and Fairview at Washington Duke. More college-priced places include Cosmic Cantina, Jimmy Johns, or Blue Corn Cafe."

Q "Off-campus restaurants are either **overpriced or of low quality** . . . drive just a bit and you'll find good restaurants on 15-501 or Chapel Hill."

Q "The **restaurants around Durham are great.** With your points account, you can also order off-campus food to be delivered to your dorm. Some good off-campus eateries include International Delights (Middle-Eastern food and Philly steaks), George's Garage (highly expensive, but very good), Jimmy John's Subs, and Satisfaction (food from the grill and pizza). Additionally, Cosmic Cantina, which is not on the points system, is also a good place to go and get Mexican food, even late at night."

Q "Ninth St. restaurants are great. **Banh's is cheap and good.**"

Q "There are a few really nice restaurants just off-campus. **There's a Greek place that is phenomenal.** AnotherThyme is another really good but pricey place, as is the restaurant at the Washington-Duke golf course and hotel. There are a few more trendy places, but I don't hit those too often. Of course, there is a Macaroni Grill, Red Lobster, Chili's, Applebee's, and Outback all within a five-minute-drive."

Q "I hardly go off-campus to eat because **I have an abundance of food points.** Students can order from some restaurants off campus and charge the food on our food points, so that's the only time I really eat off campus."

The College Prowler Take On...
Off-Campus Dining

All right, so maybe Durham doesn't have many restaurants where you walk into the dim, smoky interior and sit down at a table etched with the musings of generations past to eat some of the most exquisite food the world has to offer. A unique and time-honored college atmosphere is often lacking in some of the local eateries. This is not to say that you can't find a diamond in the rough here and there in Durham, because there are quaint little restaurants on 9th Street, such as Elmo's and Cinelli's that are loved by students throughout the Triangle area. Admittedly, a lot of students rarely travel far off-campus for much of their dining (though this may be as much a product of Duke's seclusion as is the quality of food), but there are rewards for those who choose to venture out into the wide world of Raleigh-Durham and Chapel Hill to explore the tastes.

The primary chain restaurants are available in Durham as well as the unique, regional establishments, so there's no shortage of places to eat. Finding somewhere fun is seldom a problem for Duke students. Be willing to try somewhere new—and don't spend all your time counting calories. The South is the home of soul food, and you'll regret it someday if you don't live a little and dig in.

C+

The College Prowler™ Grade on
Off-Campus Dining: C+

"A high off campus dining grade implies that off campus restaurants are affordable, accessible, and worth visiting. Other factors include the variety of cuisine and the availability of alternative options (vegetarian, vegan, kosher, etc.)"

Campus Housing

The Lowdown On...
Campus Housing

Room Types:
Duke offers single, double, and triple rooms in the residence halls, and one-, two-, and three- bedroom apartments on Central Campus. A few residence halls offer semi-private bathrooms.

Best Dorms:
Most people love the West Eden's Link, which has the largest rooms and is air-conditioned. However, others would rather stay on the main quad. On the main quads, the dorms are pretty much the same.

Worst Dorms:
Southgate, Gilbert-Addoms, Edens

Dormitory Residences:

Craven Quad
Floors: 4
Total Occupancy: 280
Bathrooms: Communal
Co-Ed: Yes
Percentage of First-Year Students: None
Room Types: Single, Double
Special Features: Laundry, Study Lounge, Arcade

Crowell Quad
Floors: 5
Total Occupancy: 265
Bathrooms: Communal
Co-Ed: Yes
Percentage of First-Year Students: None
Room Types: Single, Double, Triple
Special Features: Laundry, Study Lounge, Arcade

Edens Quad, 1A
Floors: 4
Total Occupancy: 88
Bathrooms: Communal
Co-Ed: Yes
Percentage of First-Year Students: None
Room Types: Single, Double
Special Features: Laundry, Study Lounge, Computer Lab

Edens Quad, 1B
Floors: 4
Total Occupancy: 47
Bathrooms: Communal
Co-Ed: Yes
Percentage of First-Year Students: None
Room Types: Single, Double
Special Features: A/C

Edens Quad, 1C
Floors: 4
Total Occupancy: 98
Bathrooms: Communal
Co-Ed: Yes
Percentage of First-Year Students: None
Room Types: Single, Double
Special Features: A/C

Edens Quad, 2A
Floors: 5
Total Occupancy: 88
Bathrooms: Communal
Co-Ed: Yes
Percentage of First-Year Students: None
Room Types: Double, Single
Special Features: Computer Lab, Laundry, Study Lounge

Edens Quad, 2C
Floors: 4
Total Occupancy: 99
Bathrooms: Communal
Co-Ed: Yes
Percentage of First-Year Students: None
Room Types: Single, Double
Special Features: A/C

Few Quad
Floors: 6
Total Occupancy: 500
Bathrooms: Communal
Co-Ed: Yes
Percentage of First-Year Students: None
Room Types: Single, Double
Special Features: Pac Man

Kilgo Quad
Floors: 5 plus basement
Total Occupancy: 355
Bathrooms: Communal
Co-Ed: Yes
Percentage of First-Year-Students: None
Room Types: Single, Double
Special Features: Laundry, Study Lounge

Schaefer House
Floors: 4
Total Occupancy: 144
Bathrooms: Communal
Co-Ed: Yes
Percentage of First-Year Students: None
Room Types: Single, Double
Special Features: Laundry, Study Lounge, Piano Room

Wannamaker Quad
Floors: 4 plus basement
Total Occupancy: 250
Bathrooms: Communal
Co-Ed: Yes
Percentage of First-Year Students: None
Room Types: Single, Double, Triple
Special Features: Laundry, Study Room

WEL (West Edens Link) Quad
Floors: 8
Total Occupancy: about 220
Bathrooms: Communal
Co-Ed: Yes
Percentage of First-Year Students: None
Room Types: Single, Double
Special Features: Laundry, Alcove, Study Lounge

Housing Options:

After Freshman year, Duke offers students the opportunity of "linking" to other quads, and "blocking" with a group of friends. Students who sign up to "link" will move with other students from their dorm to a selected quad on West Campus. Each East Campus dorm has a West Campus quad to which it is linked. Students who "block" are assigned consecutive numbers in the housing lottery so that they will have a better chance of living next to each other.

(Editor's note: All of the dorms listed above are on west campus. As a freshman, you will be living on East Campus, and do not have the option to choose where you live.)

Undergrads on Campus:
86%

Number of Dormitories:
Thirteen residential halls on East Campus; six residential Quads on West Campus

Number of University-Owned Apartments:
407 apartment units for undergraduates and 117 for graduate students

Bed Type:
Twin extra long (39"x80"); some beds can be bunked. Students build or buy their own lofts.

Cleaning Service?
Yes. Halls, commons rooms, and public bathrooms are cleaned daily. Your room, however, is up to you.

Available for Rent:
Micro-fridges are available for rent. If you enroll at Duke, you will receive a brochure with all sorts of equipment available for your dorm.

You Get:
Bed, Desk, Over-desk bookshelf, Dresser, Wardrobe or closet, Phone, Internet jacks

Also Available:
All dorms are smoke-free.

Substance-free housing is available for freshman year.

Language dorms, special-interest housing, and selective living groups are available after freshman year.

Students Speak Out On...
Campus Housing

"Most of the dorms here are decent. I can't think of any bad ones, and you really won't have a choice anyway."

Q "Most dorms on East are just about the same, aside from the newly air-conditioned Blackwell and Randolph and the remotely isolated Southgate. **Everything on West is air-conditioned except for Craven and Kilgo.** I would advise new students to avoid Edens. It has the smallest rooms and the longest walk to the rest of campus. Double rooms are the most common, and they average around 200 sq. ft. If you're looking for the biggest rooms, you can find them in the WEL (West-Edens Link.)"

Q "**Randolph and Blackwell are the nicest, newest dorms,** but they're the smallest. The others are older but have more space."

Q "**Dorms are very nice!** Most of the rooms are huge! However, as a freshman, avoid Southgate and try to get a place at the main quad on East Campus—Brown, Pegram, Jiles, Wilson, Bassett, etc."

Q "Dorms are in the process of being improved, but for the most part **they're all nice—small, but nice.** They range on size and some are in very good locations on the main quad."

Q "All the dorms seemed nice. They were fairly clean and **the rooms weren't tremendously small.** Definitely try to get in an air-conditioned dorm if possible."

Q "The **dorms are pretty nice at Duke.** You're randomly assigned to a place for your freshman year. After that, there is a housing lottery in which upperclassmen get the first shot at choosing rooms. The air-conditioned rooms on east campus are a bit smaller than the others, but beyond that trade-off, they're much the same. There's not really a dorm to avoid, even if you could."

Q "A new dorm was just built that is really nice. **The East Campus dorms aren't air conditioned,** but you don't really need it. All of the rooms are pretty similar, so I wouldn't worry about it. The rooms are pretty good-sized as well."

Q "I find that **the plan of having all first year students on East Campus is a good idea**, and it allows the new students to be together and share new experiences. I didn't hear about any particularly terrible dorms, except that Southgate is far from many facilities. On West, Edens is the trap to avoid, because it is miles away from any known civilization."

Q "Dorms on east campus aren't air-conditioned, save for two. Rooms in the air-conditioned dorms are between 140 and 160 square feet, while rooms in the other dorms are between 170 and 220 square feet. I lived in Southgate this year, and while it's kind of geographically isolated, **that isolation fosters a great sense of dorm unity.** Dorms are small, and never have more than 150 kids or so."

Q "I'm really considering an apartment for junior year because I'd like to have more personal space than in a dorm, but a lot of people like being on West because everything happens there. **Central is less convenient,** but buses run every fifteen minutes to take people to or from their apartments, so it's not too bad."

Q "I'm in Alspaugh, which is a dorm right on the green, and I love it. **Our room is small, but the location is wonderful.** We're right next to the library, across from the Marketplace and in the center of everything else. Pretty much everyone loves their dorm, so I wouldn't say there's any to avoid."

Q "**The dorms at Duke are normal dorms.** They are not anything to get excited about. Some of them have no AC, which is bad. The dorms on the quad look really cool. It would be really neat to live in them for the first week thinking to yourself, 'Wow! I can't believe I am living in this great, gothic building in the heart of campus.' Then, in the second and all subsequent weeks, 'Wow. I can't believe how hot it is in this tiny #*#@in room.'"

Q "The one dorm students typically avoided, **Trent, has been closed as a dormitory.** The non-renovated dorms on main west campus feel a bit cramped in the hallways, but the rooms themselves are nice. Regarding distance from bus stops and classes, Edens is worth avoiding."

Q "Some things are nice about the dorms, but some things definitely aren't. **On East Campus, the laundry machines are really pathetic,** although I hear they get better on West. However, we do have housekeeping staff that clean the bathrooms and halls every weekday. A lot of the dorms don't have air-conditioning (unless you have a medical reason to need AC; then they'll rent you a window unit), although I know the administration is working to change that."

Q "Freshman year nobody has a lot of choice in where to live, but students can request an air-conditioned, single-sex (by hall), or substance-free dorm. **I really recommend the substance-free dorm,** where I lived. It's a lot cleaner, and I really liked not having to deal with drunken people. After freshman year, most people just try to avoid Edens Quad because it's farther away from the main part of the campus than all the other quads."

The College Prowler Take On...
Campus Housing

Duke has some pretty nice housing, all in all. However, there are some notable differences between old and new dorms. The view from the older dorms on the main quads is spectacular, and it's nice to be close to the action. Old East Campus dorms have hardwood floors and oddly shaped rooms, while old West Campus dorms are tiled and even more oddly shaped. None of the older dorms on East Campus have air conditioning, which can make it pretty miserable for a few summer months. On West Campus, however, renovations have updated most of the rooms on the main quad and added a/c. The newer dorms, meanwhile, are homogenous, shiny, and air-conditioned but lack that old-world charm. Finally, there is Central. Central Campus is essentially a vast spread of student apartments, separated from the action on both of the main quads, but allowing students to have their own bedroom and share a kitchen and living room. The décor is shabby 70's, but if you like cooking your own food, Central holds obvious benefits.

Students agree that there are very few dorms on Duke's campus that really ought to be avoided. The tradeoff is usually pretty simple: classic beauty on one of the main quads, air conditioning and brand-spanking-newness in one of the newer dorms, or a level of autonomy. One thing's for sure, whichever dorm you choose, it will grow on you.

The College Prowler™ Grade on
Campus Housing: B

"A high Campus Housing grade indicates that dorms are clean, well-maintained and spacious. Other determining factors include variety of dorms, proximity to classes and social atmosphere."

Off-Campus Housing

The Lowdown On...
Off-Campus Housing

Average Rent for a Studio Apartment:
$430/month

Average Rent for a One-Bedroom Apartment:
$560/month

Average Rent for a Two-Bedroom Apartment:
$720/month

Popular Areas:
Duke Villa
Duke Manor
The Belmont
Buchanan Blvd.

For Assistance Contact:
Duke Community Housing
Web: www.communityhousing.duke.edu
Phone: (919) 660-1785
Email: communityhousing@duke.edu

Students Speak Out On...
Off-Campus Housing

> "The housing isn't awful, but I live in a tiny apartment. It's nothing like the city, but what else is there?"

Q "We don't have much of a choice in regards to off-campus housing. **The lottery system keeps getting worse** every year for upperclassmen, but we're required to live on campus for three years. Freshmen might have the best situation as far as housing is concerned."

Q "I have a couple of friends moving off-campus next year, and **they all seemed to find decent places without much trouble.** I couldn't really tell you though, because I'll be spending all four years on campus."

Q "Well, considering **you have to live on campus for three years,** this is almost a non-issue. Everyone lives on campus until they are seniors. For some reason, the seniors all go live in the same dumpy apartment complexes right off-campus."

Q "**I wouldn't recommend living in the apartment complexes closest to campus,** as crime has been a problem. I am moving about ten minutes away from campus, and the new apartment complexes there are really nice."

Q "It's very convenient, but you have to drive four to five minutes to campus for class everyday; and remember, **there's very little parking.**"

Q "I didn't have any trouble finding an apartment, but **rent is very, very high.**"

Q "Students are required to live on campus for three out of the four years, and, after that, there are houses and apartments that are fairly close to the campus. However, since **they aren't that close,** students must drive to school and parking, again, is really bad."

Q "Housing off-campus is easy. **Most seniors live off-campus** and drive or take the bus to school."

Q "How convenient is off-campus housing? **You can't live off campus your freshman year.** Or your sophomore year. Or your junior year. Where's the convenience in that!"

Q "Most students live on campus (about eighty percent, I think), but **houses or apartments off-campus aren't too hard to find.** Parking is the only problem. Freshman year, you'll live on east campus with all of the other freshmen, and then you'll move to dorms on west campus or to apartments on central campus for the rest of your time there (unless you really want to move off-campus)."

Q "It depends where you have your apartment. **In most cases, you need a car.** After your first or second year, you can also rent an apartment on the grad campus (central campus)."

Q "Housing off-campus is **only an option as a senior,** as students are required to live on campus through their junior year. As a senior, housing opportunities are quite diverse, ranging from townhouses to apartments to full houses."

Q "Well, **we have to live on campus for three years.** But I know that a lot of people who choose to live off campus after that seem to live in the neighborhood surrounding East which isn't all that safe. So I guess there are advantages and disadvantages in that department."

Q "It **doesn't make sense to live off-campus after freshman year.** The university has an uncanny ability to provide housing for everyone who needs it. While you only have to live on campus for three years, the Central Campus apartments are nicer and less expensive than apartments in the RTP area, I would suspect. The only catch to living on campus is that you may not always get what you'd like from the room selection."

Q "We're all required to live on campus for three years: freshman year in a dorm on East Campus, sophomore year in a dorm on West Campus, and junior year either on West again or in an apartment on Central Campus. Senior year, students can do whatever they want for housing. **Housing seems to be pretty readily available near campus,** and I'd say that it would definitely be worth it for anyone wanting to save some money on housing costs."

The College Prowler Take On...
Off-Campus Housing

Since you really can't even start thinking about living off-campus till you're done with your junior year, most students don't worry about it too much. However, if you're a big "I want my own apartment, off-campus, far away from campus, with neighbors who call the police frequently, and I want it now!" kind of person, you might have problems with Duke. However, you might be pleased when you consider that Duke really does have reasonable housing, really close to classes.

You might also consider the fact that when you're running away from Duke's campus you're not really running to all that much. Off-campus housing really isn't the exciting cosmopolitan experience it might be in other colleges, which goes back to the problem with local atmosphere. Unfortunately, a lot of the apartments around Duke are small, plain, and overpriced.

The College Prowler™ Grade on Off-Campus Housing: C-

A high grade in Off-Campus Housing indicates that apartments are of high quality, close to campus, affordable, and easy to secure.

Diversity

The Lowdown On...
Diversity

Breakdown:

Asian, Asian-American, or Pacific Islander:
15.1%

African-American/Black:
10.3%

Hispanic/Latino:
7.3%

Native American, American Indian, Native Alaskan, or Native Hawaiian:
.2%

Caucasian:
67%

Percentage of students from various regions:

Carolinas: 14%

Northeast: 15%

Mid-Atlantic: 20%

Southeast: 23%

Midwest: 12%

West and Pacific: 9%

International: 7%

Political Activity:
Duke, like most colleges, has a strong liberal streak, but conservatives have made their voices heard as well. Students campaign for various political candidates, and two students set up a system which paid students to drive low-income Durham residents to the polls for the 2004 presidential election. In 2003 there were sit-ins, rallies, and marches to protest the war in Iraq.

Gay Tolerance:
The gay scene is not very visible at Duke, but gays are not generally singled out for persecution, despite Princeton Review's recent slight of Duke as "the most gay unfriendly campus in the United States." A recent campaign for gay acceptance handed out shirts reading "Gay? Fine by me?" and met with an enthusiastic response as students across campus lined up to get the shirts—the 2,000 they had ordered quickly ran out.

Most Popular Religions:
The spires of Duke chapel dominate the West Campus view, but in the basement of the chapel, Duke's Religious Life center funds and promotes many of the religions most prominent on campus, including Protestant, Catholic, Jewish, Muslim, and Hindu faiths. The Freeman Center for Jewish Life provides a location for Jewish activities, and Duke Chapel hosts Protestant meetings every Sunday, but many congregations meet off campus. Religious groups of all sorts are active on Duke's campus, making their presence felt and their interests heard.

Economic Status:
The Duke Student body is astoundingly wealthy. Even those who are on financial aid usually manage to look, shop, and drive rich. There are, of course, people from a variety of economic backgrounds, but you wouldn't think it to look at the campus. Duke is remarkably image-conscious.

Minority Clubs:
Duke has a number of thriving minority clubs, which put on astounding cultural programs each year. Perhaps one of the most active is SAASA, the South-Asian American Student Association, which involves most of the South-Asian Students on Campus. The ASA (Asian Student Association) is also a vibrant part of the community.

Students Speak Out On...
Diversity

> "The majority of Duke students are White and middle or upper class. There is still a fairly significant minority presence on campus, but many ethnic groups tend to stick together and become somewhat cliquish."

Q "There are **definitely black parties and white parties**. That said, racial and socioeconomic differences shouldn't get in the way of your friendships."

Q "It's a **diverse campus**. There are students from just about every background you can think of."

Q "The campus isn't really all that diverse, and **everyone tends, initially, to stick to their own,** which kind of sucks. I came from a high school where the white/black mix was about 60/40, but at Duke, it seems that rich, white kids are the norm, and there isn't much in the way of anyone else."

Q "The campus is quite diverse but **people tend to self-segregate themselves.** There has been a lot of work at the school to promote inter-racial relations, and there's definitely the option of meeting all sorts of people."

Q "The campus is **not very diverse at all.** There may be a lot of different races on campus, but everyone is coming from the same upper class, New England culture. So everyone likes the same music, sees the same movies, wears the same clothing, uses the same slang, etc. It's frightening really."

Q "The **majority of the study body is white.** I think that around 60% of students are white and the rest are black, Hispanic, Asian, etc."

Q "The campus is rather diverse and largely self-segregated. Even in the cafeteria you'll see **the black tables, the Asian tables, and the White tables**. This greatly concerns the administration, and they try to change it, which we pretty much agree is stupid and not their place to do so."

Q "If you desire diversity, you will have it, especially if you get involved in a sport or another activity. **I have made black friends, Asian friends, and white friends.** We also have students from other countries, including my friend's Pakistani resident assistant and the cute Venezuelan girl in my French class. Aside from just the racial or ethnic standpoint, I think Duke students come from varied backgrounds and upbringings and have a lot to share, even if it's just that South Dakota accent or an appreciation of grits with ketchup."

Q "I'd say the campus is diverse. **There are a lot of different minorities represented**, and it's about a 50-50 split between guys and girls."

Q "My class at Duke incorporates students from 44 countries, and one third of the students are non-white. **I'd call that diversity.**"

Q "I think it's like twenty-five percent minority, maybe more. There are some problems with **people only hanging out with people of their own race**, but I've never seen any racism, and, personally, I've made friends with people from lots of different backgrounds and races."

Q "Ethnically, it is very diverse. **Socio-economically, I'm not so sure...**"

Q "**The school is very diverse.** That is part of their [administration's] mission. You'll find almost every race somewhere at Duke. That's a good thing too, because everyone gets along really well."

Q "It seems fairly diverse to me in terms of race, political views, religion, etc. And **everyone seems fairly tolerant of others' differences.**"

Q "Compared to other schools of the same caliber, Duke is very diverse in student body. **Students of color make up a third of the campus** and are actively involved. There was a lot of segregation in the housing system but administration stepped up and changed housing policies with the intentions of getting people across the race lines to communicate."

Q "As part of the first sophomore class forced to live on West Campus, I was able to observe how much better people of different races got along when their living situation was similar to their freshmen year. I lived with most of the same people from my freshmen dorm and **it allowed us to get closer** instead of losing them somewhere in the social scene after my first year was over (that's what usually happens). Diversity in the faculty is something to work on in the future."

The College Prowler Take On...
Diversity

How do you define diversity? Though it may not be the most diverse campus in the world, Duke does have a thriving community of students from almost every ethnic background. However, Duke students tend to segregate themselves and hang out with their own ethnic group. This is not always the case, of course, but a number of students seem to have a group of mixed-race friends, and then another group of friends from their own racial background. This is a little worrisome, but the administration's concern over the issue should prove that they're at least trying to remedy this. Most students feel that there's not much to be done about it.

There is also the issue of economic background. Here. Duke is remarkably homogenous. Duke students are almost all rich, or at least rich-looking. This is not to say that everyone owns a yacht and plays golf with their dads' business buddies on the weekend, nor that students are obnoxious with their wealth, but you will want to be aware of this before you come to Duke. You might even want to make a stop at Abercrombie on the way to Durham.

B+

The College Prowler™ Grade on
Diversity: B+

A high grade in Diversity indicates that ethnic minorities and international students have a notable presence on campus, and that students of different economic backgrounds, religious beliefs, and sexual preferences are well-represented.

Guys & Girls

The Lowdown On...
Guys & Girls

Women Undergrads:
49%

Men Undergrads:
51%

Birth Control Available?
Yes. Duke Student Health offers a variety of contraceptive options, and condoms are available in all the dorm vending machines.

Hookups or Relationships?
Relationships seem to require a fair amount of effort to keep up, and there seems to be a limited amount of effort that hard working Duke students are willing to give. So, although you will still find a number of students committed to each other and their relationships, hookups are the order of the weekend.

Social Scene:

It is a rare student who doesn't find Duke a bit cliquish. This is not to say that you can't make a lot of friends in a variety of groups, but sometimes Duke can feel like high school revisited. Students are fun, bright, and attractive, but tend to stay in small groups of fun, bright, and attractive people. It is easy to carry on a conversation with classmates on the bus, walking to or from a class, or anywhere on campus, but if you're from different groups it is unlikely you will make many friends out of your casual acquaintances.

However, Duke can still be a lot of fun once you find your group of friends. Dorms, clubs, organizations, and projects—anything where you work with a lot with other people—can be great places to make strong friendships.

Dress Code

There is no set dress code but, overall, students dress "preppy." A&F reigns supreme, with button-up shirts, logo T-shirts, khakis, and New Balances being a part of nearly every student's wardrobe. Duke students almost always look good, and you will find few who are willing to roll out of bed and go to class in their pajamas. Usually students are tastefully dressed, looking like they just stepped off the page of some magazine or other, although there is the occasional girl who doesn't seem to know how much is enough. Despite all the attractiveness you may find yourself gazing longingly after the one or two people who have dared disapproval and bedecked their backpacks with pins, pierced an eyebrow, or let their hair grow out.

Did You Know?
Best Place to Meet Guys/Girls:
- The Quads
- Classes
- Parties

Students Speak Out On...
Guys & Girls

> "The majority of people at Duke are very attractive and very career-oriented. There isn't much time or interest in starting serious relationships, so most don't make it past the weekend—which opens doors to getting to meet new people."

Q "The guys aren't particularly hot, but the athletes are okay. The girls are alright, but **they seem goody-goody sometimes.**"

Q "Well, I'm a guy, so I can tell you that **the girls are mediocre.** I find a lot of people at Duke to be a little introverted, so it's kind of hard to approach women, at least when sobriety is involved. Take that for what it's worth."

Q "Most of the students look like they **just walked out of a J.Crew catalog.**"

Q "A lot of students here are cute, but **there are very few of them that would get a 'ten.'** According to my best friends who are guys, they complain about the girls here. They are constantly hoping the next freshman class will be prettier."

Q "I heard Fox was going to do a reality show on campus titled, '**Rich Dorks Turned Cool.**' You have to dig deep to find the down-to-earth people here."

Q "Let's just say **you'll have your choice of hot guys.**"

Q "**There aren't enough good-looking girls at Duke**, so if you're hot, please, please, please come to Duke!"

Q "There are some good looking gals, but **most of them know it and are kind of stuck up about it.** The best girls are cute and down-to-earth. Most of the guys keep in pretty good shape; I see a whole bunch in the gym everyday. Almost everybody runs and takes care of themselves."

Q "Hah! Given the typical upper-middle class origins of most students, most are attractive. In all seriousness, **the guys here are more often attractive than the girls.** I kid you not."

Q "The guys on campus are for the most part good looking. **They seem to be nice** and willing to help, as do the girls."

Q "At Duke, you got your hot ones, you got your nice ones, and you got your 'others.' A nice plus is that although all Duke girls do not rank a perfect ten, **many have great personalities and very interesting conversation skills,** and that ends up being more important, right?"

Q "Basically, it's pretty diverse, so there are all kinds of people here from all over. It makes a pretty good mix. The specifics, well, **you'll have to come and see for yourself.**"

Q "Duke is full of beautiful people. Everywhere. There's some concern that **a lot of the girls have eating disorders.** In certain groups, personal appearance is a big deal, though there are always the dissenters."

Q "The student body itself is pretty cool, and for being a highly academic school we have some really good looking kids—**the guys are hot, anyway!**"

Q "You'll meet different types of people depending on how you decide to spend your time. I like to think **there's plenty of variety around.**"

Q "The guys are all dorks. They all have an attitude of trying to be cool, party, frat guys even though **they're all really geeks at heart.**"

Q "The girls and guys who I know are really fun, and we have a good time together, even if we do drive each other crazy when we're cooped up in the dorms for too long. **There are a lot of attractive people on campus**, but I don't pay a lot of attention to that because I have a boyfriend and don't feel like I should be looking. From what I've heard, the dating scene is pretty dead (although hooking up is popular)."

The College Prowler Take On...
Guys & Girls

Duke students are a pretty attractive bunch on the whole, and go to great lengths to be viewed that way. Guys seem to get more praise than girls, at least in physical attractiveness. Girls, however, are not at all unattractive, and the main complaints seem to be about introverted and sometimes shallow personalities. A lot of the students seem to have gotten a bit too caught up in their appearance to worry about personality and relationships. This correlates with the dating scene at Duke. Students are much more likely to have a nice little Friday night hookup than to build a lasting relationship. After all, why put effort into finding something real and substantial if you can have what you're looking for with no strings attached?

It's important to remember that although Duke students are generally attractive, image-conscious, and rich, they're also generally smart. Usually, school comes before relationships, but you've got to keep yourself looking good for those few exceptions.

B+

The College Prowler™ Grade on Guys: B+

A high grade for Guys indicates that the male population on campus is attractive, smart, friendly, and engaging, and that the school has a decent ratio of guys to girls.

B

The College Prowler™ Grade on Girls: B

A high grade for Girls not only implies that the women on campus are attractive, smart, friendly, and engaging, but also that there is a fair ratio of girls to guys.

Athletics

The Lowdown On...
Athletics

Athletic Division:
Division 1A

Conference:
ACC
(Atlantic Coast Conference)

Intercollegiate Varsity Sports

Men's Teams:
Baseball, Basketball, Cross Country, Fencing, Football, Golf, Lacrosse, Soccer, Swimming, Tennis, Track, Wrestling

Women's Teams:
Basketball, Cross Country, Fencing, Field Hockey, Golf, Lacrosse, Rowing, Soccer, Swimming, Tennis, Track, Volleyball,

→

Club Sports:
Badminton, Ballroom Dance, Baseball, Women's Basketball, Men's Crew, Cycling, Dancing Devils, Equestrian, Field Hockey, Football, Golf, Hapkido, Ice Hockey, Judo, Women's Lacrosse, Outing, Roadrunners, Roller Hockey, Men's Rugby, Women's Rugby, Sailing, Skating, Shooting, Ski, Men's Soccer, Women's Soccer, Softball, Squash, Swim, Table Tennis, Tae Kwon Do, Men's Tennis, Women's Tennis, Men's Ultimate, Women's Ultimate, Men's Volleyball, Women's Volleyball, Water Ski

Intramurals:
First-year only: Six-a-Side Soccer, Flag Football, Basketball, Co-Rec Basketball, Volleyball, Softball,

Regular: Flag Football, Soccer, Volleyball, Singles & Doubles Tennis, Golf, 5k Run, Basketball, Squash, Racquetball, Badminton, Co-Rec Basketball, Softball, Table Tennis

Athletic Fields

Jack Coombs Field – Baseball

Cameron Indoor Stadium – Basketball

Schwartz-Butters Athletic Center

Wallace Wade Stadium – Football

The Duke Golf Club – Golf

Koskinen Stadium – Lacrosse and Soccer

Taishoff Aquatic Center – Swimming and Diving

Ambler Tennis Stadium/Sheffield Indoor Tennis Center – Tennis

Wallace Wade Stadium – Track and Field

Memorial Gym – Volleyball

School Mascot:
Blue Devil

Getting Tickets:

Students get into Duke games for free, and getting in is usually not a problem. For example, you can walk up to the football stadium during halftime, and you'll be sure to get in free. The same is certainly not true for men's basketball. The stories you have heard of people camping out for months to get tickets are not in the least exaggerated. Students form groups and plan schedules around being able to sleep in a tent from January to late February/Early March. You can usually get into basketball games even if you don't camp out, but the best seats will surely be gone, and you will still have to get there several hours early to wait in line.

Most Popular Sports

Men's Basketball. Take a smart-kid school, add one really exceptional sports team, and it will become the Mecca around which we all flock.

Overlooked Teams:

Women's basketball is not necessarily overlooked, but it is certainly hard for it to get the attention it deserves; especially considering that Duke has some of the nation's top players. The lacrosse team is also choice, and hardly gets the credit it deserves.

Best Place to Take a Walk

Sarah P. Duke Gardens. They are astoundingly beautiful. Duke Forest may be tempting, but don't ever try it alone. Of course, everywhere on Duke campus is beautiful, so even the walk from East to West can be enjoyable.

Gyms/Facilities

Wilson Recreation Center

This new facility is filled with everything students need to keep in shape, including free weights, weight machines, a pool, squash courts, exercise machines, and classrooms for aerobics and Pilates. The building is so well equipped that you will almost never have a problem finding a machine to use, and the novelty of the facility and equipment will get you excited from the moment you step through the door

Brodie Recreation Center

Brodie is East Campus's fitness facility, and is older and smaller than its West Campus counterpart. However, it offers all of the basics including free weights and weight machines, a pool, exercise machines, and basketball courts. Although Wilson is newer, nicer, and bigger, Brodie offers a much more convenient facility for east campus residents.

Tennis Courts

East and West Campuses both offer tennis courts next to the gyms. The IM building (next to Wilson) has indoor tennis courts.

Students Speak Out On...
Athletics

> "Duke has some of the top ranked sports on campus. Being a basketball fanatic is key and even if you're not now, you'll eventually start seeing blue after a while. It's hard not to catch the school's basketball fever."

Q "Duke football is the worst, but **people still go to games for school spirit** and social activities**.** Basketball games are, of course, the most popular."

Q "Men's basketball is huge. Besides academics, **Duke is known for men's basketball.** I don't know if you have heard about K-Ville, but K-Ville is where all the students camp out for weeks to get tickets to the games."

Q "We're all nicknamed 'Cameron Crazies.' **Mostly everyone at Duke is crazy about b-ball.** If you ever get the chance to go to a game, it's crazy. Nobody sits down. You stand the whole time. It's a great thing to experience. Women's golf is also a huge sport at Duke. I'm on the golf team. We are the ACC champs for the seventh year in a row, and the 1999 NCAA champs. We are going back to NCAA this year and we're looking to take home the title!"

Q "It's awesome! Words can't describe how great it is to experience the Duke basketball team; I never followed college basketball, and now I'm a die-hard fan. **IM sports are prevalent, too.**"

Q "We love our basketball. Come to Duke, and **you'll understand what it is to be a Cameron Crazy** and what it's like to camp out in the cold in order to score access to big games such as those against our dreaded rivals, Maryland and UNC. You just might also see a national championship, too. However, after 23 consecutive losses, we've pretty much given up on football. Although I haven't participated in intramurals, I hear they're pretty intense."

Q "**Ever heard of Duke basketball?** Yeah, it's big. It's fun. It's what makes Duke students spend a week in tents in the cold. As for other sports, there's our football team, which has only won a handful of games since 1999. We also have a pretty good volleyball team; and there's girls' crew, men's lacrosse, baseball, soccer, and everything you'd expect."

Q "There are lots of groups involved in IM sports, including frat and sorority teams as well as dorms, selective houses, and some extracurricular activity groups. **I think the marching band even has an IM softball team.**"

Q "Varsity sports are big here, of course headlined by basketball. **Students participate in bonfires on campus after big wins,** and the basketball team is the rallying point for much school spirit. As freshmen, many IM sports are organized by dorm, contributing to a sense of unity, rather than anonymity. IM football, softball, volleyball, and basketball are the most prevalent. Duke also has club teams, which are relaxed teams for intercollegiate competition. Some examples include Ultimate Frisbee, tennis, volleyball, and football."

Q "Varsity sports, and by that I mostly mean basketball, are crazy-big at Duke. If you get into all the nonsense, you'll wind up spending daily shifts in a tent outside of Cameron Indoor Stadium just to get into certain games. (This is actually a lot of fun. It's a tent city of drunken madness!) **Our football team really sucks,** so I wouldn't bother with that, but the soccer and lacrosse teams are really good and fun to watch."

Q "**Basketball, basketball, basketball.** Men's reigns, but the women are popular too. Football is not big unless you have some free time to kill. Men's soccer and tennis are popular too. I don't know anything about the IM sports (unless crew is one of them, not sure)."

Q "**Duke oozes with school spirit,** especially during basketball season. If you're not a basketball fan before coming to Duke, you will be; if you're already a basketball fan, Duke basketball will accelerate your interest to obsession status. Other teams do have a following on campus—lacrosse for example—but the big name sport on other campuses, football, is more than lacking at Duke. IM sports are widespread, though not publicized well."

Q "Of course, Duke basketball is huge! We have a great men's team, as everyone knows, but **I like to watch the women play even more**, and right now they're doing better than the men are. Other sports are less popular, but we have really good women's volleyball and field hockey teams. Watching sports isn't my favorite entertainment, but there's plenty for anyone to go see. I haven't really heard a lot about IM sports."

The College Prowler Take On...
Athletics

Have you ever heard of Duke basketball? If you haven't, then you must have been living under a rock for the last twenty years! The current of basketball fanaticism pulses through everyone and everything at Duke. You see a ridiculously tall guy get on the bus, and the eyes of the students all around you light up. You notice the strain on their faces as they try to hold themselves back from running up and asking for an autograph. This is not to say that you have to be a basketball fan before you come here—Duke will most definitely make one out of you.

Ironically, the classic college sport, football, is just laughable at Duke. However, the other varsity and IM sports make a better-than-decent showing each year, and there's a good team for just about everyone out here. Mostly, though, there's basketball. Come, and let us make you a fan.

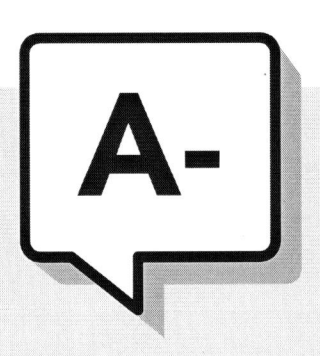

A-

The College Prowler™ Grade on
Athletics: A-

A high grade in athletics indicates that students have school spirit, that sports programs are respected, that games are well-attended, and that intramurals are a prominent part of student life.

Nightlife

The Lowdown On...
Nightlife

Club and Bar Prowler: Popular Nightlife Spots!

Bars Close At:
2:00 am

Primary Areas with Nightlife:
Durham has a fair number of clubs and bars, but some of them can feel rather seedy. George's, on Ninth Street, is an exception and manages to feel upscale in all its facets. Chapel Hill's Franklin Street has more of the college feel and is not terribly over-priced.

Bars/ Clubs In the Durham/Chapel Hill Area:

Carolina Brewery and Restaurant
460 W Franklin St
Chapel Hill, NC 27516
Phone: (919) 942-1800
Price: $21-30
Hours: Sunday-Tuesday 11:30 a.m.-12 a.m.; Wednesday-Thursday 11:30 a.m.-1 a.m.; Friday-Saturday 11:30 a.m.-2 a.m.

Charlie's Neighborhood Bar
758 9th St
Durham, NC 27705
Phone: (919) 286-4446

Duke Coffeehouse
Crowell Building, East Campus
Duke University
Durham, NC 27706
Phone: (919) 684-4069
Price: No cover during the day, usually $5 for bands
Hours: Monday-Friday 9 a.m.-12 a.m. Saturday 10:30 a.m.-2 a.m. Sunday 9 a.m.-12 a.m.

The Edge
108 Morris St
Durham, NC 27701
Phone: (919) 667-1012
Hours: Tuesday 8 p.m.-11 p.m.; Thursday 8 p.m.-12 a.m.; Friday 5 p.m.-2:30 a.m., Saturday 9:45 p.m.-2:30 a.m.

Forty-Eight Hours Bar & Billiards
2825 Roxboro St
Durham, NC 27704-3245
Phone: (919) 317-1600
Minimum Age: 21

George's Garage
Food: Mediterranean, Seafood bar and grill, bakery, to-go food market
Address: 737 Ninth Street
Phone: (919) 286-4131
Price: $21 to $30
Hours: Sunday-Thursday 5 p.m.-10 p.m.; Friday-Saturday 5 p.m.-11 p.m.; Sunday Brunch 10 a.m.-2 p.m.; Bar opens at 4 p.m.
George's features live music, a bar scene, and local favorites

James Joyce Pub
912 W Main St
Durham, NC 27701
Phone: (919) 683-3022
Hours: Monday-Saturday 11:30 a.m.-2 a.m.; Sunday 12 p.m.-2 a.m.

Mug Shots & Bugsy's
746 9TH St
Durham, NC 27705-4803
Phone: (919) 416-8595

Palace International and Club Crystyle's
117 W. Parrish St
Durham, NC 27701
Phone: (919) 687-4922
Hours: Open for lunch Monday through Friday from 11 a.m. to 3 p.m.; Entertainment Friday and Saturday nights 9:30 p.m. to 3 a.m.

Player's
159 1/2 E Franklin St
Chapel Hill, NC 27514
Phone: (919) 929-0101
Hours: Thursday-Saturday 10 p.m.-2 a.m.

Ringside
308 W Main St
Durham, NC 27701
Phone: (919) 680-2100
Hours: Wednesday-Saturday 9:30 p.m.-2 a.m.

Satisfaction Restaurant and Bar
905 W Main St
Brightleaf Square
Durham, NC 27701
Phone: (919) 682-7397
Fax: (919) 683-3853
Hours: Monday-Wednesday 11 a.m.-1 a.m.; Thursday-Saturday 11 a.m.-2 a.m.

Shooter's Saloon
827 W Morgan St
Durham, NC 27701
Phone: (919) 680-0428

Talk of the Town
108 E. Main Street
Durham, NC 27701
Phone: (919) 682-7747
Price: Cover is charged for live entertainment
Hours: Tuesday-Saturday 6 p.m.-1 a.m.

Visions
711 Rigsbee Ave
Durham, NC 27701-2138
Phone: (919) 688-3002
Hours: Friday-Saturday 9 p.m.-2:30 a.m.

Favorite Drinking Games:

Beer Pong

Card Games (A$$hole)

Century Club

Quarters

Power Hour

Student Favorites:

Satisfaction

James Joyce

Carolina Brewery

Mug Shots

George's

The Edge

Shooter's

Organization Parties:

Most every student association, be it Frat or minority club, throws parties with plenty of drinking and dancing. Sometimes they are held at clubs in the area (George's is a favorite), but on-campus parties are just as common.

What to Do if You're Not 21

Many of the clubs (including George's and Duke Coffeehouse) allow eighteen-and-over, but you'll have to rely on classic college fallbacks to get a drink.

Students Speak Out On...
Nightlife

"The parties on campus range widely, and it really is hit or miss whether you get a good one or a dud. The best are the ones that the black fraternities/sororities sponsor."

Q "The **theme house and fraternity parties are great for drinking** but only sometimes have good music and dancing. I don't know much about the bars and clubs, but George's seem to be popular."

Q "It pretty much sucks here. **There are no clubs, really.** There are two to three places off-campus for those who are eighteen or older, and the other three to four places are bars. Students go to the Chapel Hill bars when we want to go out."

Q "I wouldn't worry so much about partying hard now, because you won't have much chance until you're older. **The bars are lousy**, so your own parties are the best!"

Q "**The bars and clubs in Durham are glorified dumps** that get filled up with sorority events, but they're not horrible. As long as you have a good time, the way the place looks doesn't really matter. I only recently turned twenty-one, so I haven't had time to take in the whole club scene; friends of mine seem to think it's a lot better in Chapel Hill."

Q "I'm not much for clubs, but **there are some good bars around.** The James Joyce and Satisfaction are both downtown bars. There are also several in Chapel Hill. My favorite bar there is the Carolina Brewery. They also have good food."

Q "Bars and clubs are good; **they have a bunch of bars on Ninth Street** (Mugshots, Charlie's, George's) and a group in Brightleaf Square (Satisfaction and James Joyce), but you need to be twenty-one to get in."

Q "Younger groups can get into Mugshots or George's (it's eighteen and up on one night). **Dance clubs are mostly in Chapel Hill,** which is only fifteen minutes away and has a really cool college scene."

Q "There are bars, and some within walking distance of east campus, but **we really tend to stay on campus most of the time.**"

Q "**There are always parties on the weekends**, and I'm sure it's easier to get alcohol there if you're into that, but I don't drink. Those who go clubbing usually go to Raleigh, which is maybe forty-five minutes away."

Q "The **bars and clubs off-campus are decent.** They don't hold a candle to the stuff we have at home, but they're still fun. Gotham in Chapel Hill is a favorite, as is Mug Shots and Satisfaction in downtown Durham. There is another club/restaurant called George's Garage that is really good, too."

Q "If people **want to go partying, they go to Chapel Hill**, which is very close to Durham—around ten minutes by car. I think there is a University bus going to and from Chapel Hill on weekends."

Q "There are six or eight clubs within a short distance of campus, but only a few bars. Most Duke students that want to drink at a bar choose to drive or take a bus to Chapel Hill, where **there are literally a dozen unique bars.**"

Q "**You really have to venture off-campus to find good night spots.** The campus is about five miles from any significant town, so you would be doing some minor commuting. There are, however, several nightspots (bars) once you get there. I really haven't been out too much because of the workload, since I major in law."

Q "The clubbing scene is available to those who are interested in it. Lansdowne Street has a ton of clubs for nineteen and older, but **these can get expensive fairly quickly** if you go a lot."

Q "**Bars and clubs around here are lame.** There is too much drinking and not enough Twister going on at the parties."

Q "I'm not a big partygoer myself, but for those who do like that sort of thing, **there are almost always frat parties on the weekends** (and sometimes during the week, I think). George's Garage, which is on Ninth Street, seems to be the most popular bar, and Shooters is also pretty well-liked."

The College Prowler Take On...
Nightlife

Duke's social scene involves a large amount of on campus, organization sponsored parties with copious amounts of alcohol. However, finding clubs and bars in the immediate vicinity can be difficult. Fortunately for those who must have alcohol to get a party going (which is, arguably, the case for just about every campus in America), there are an abundant number of parties happening on campus where drinks are free and no one's checking IDs. Be aware that Duke police do sometimes come to check up, and if need be, crack down on parties where underage drinking is rampant.

In Durham, there doesn't seem to be too many clubs or bars worth visiting. When you reach that great and enlightened club-and-bar-scene age, your best bet is Duke's perennial college town standby, Chapel Hill.

The College Prowler™ Grade on
Nightlife: C+

A high grade in Nightlife indicates that there are many bars and clubs in the area that are easily accessible and affordable. Other determining factors include the number of options for the under-21 crowd and the prevalence of house parties.

Greek Life

The Lowdown On...
Greek Life

Number of Fraternities:
20

Number of Sororities:
17

Percent of Undergrad Men in Fraternities:
29%

Percent of Undergrad Women in Sororities:
42%

Fraternities on Campus:
Alpha Epsilon Pi, Alpha Phi Alpha Fraternity, Inc., Alpha Tau Omega, Beta Theta Pi, Chi Psi, Delta Kappa Epsilon, Delta Sigma Phi, Kappa Alpha, Kappa Alpha Psi Fraternity, Inc., Lambda Phi Epsilon, Lambda Upsilon Lambda Fraternity, Inc., Omega Psi Phi Fraternity, Inc., Phi Beta Sigma Fraternity, Inc., Pi Kappa Alpha, Psi Upsilon (co-ed), Sigma Nu

Sororities on Campus:
Alpha Delta Pi, Alpha Epsilon Phi, Alpha Kappa Alpha Sorority, Inc., Alpha Omicron Pi, Alpha Phi, Chi Omega, Delta Delta Delta, Delta Gamma, Delta Sigma Theta Sorority, Inc., Kappa Alpha Theta, Kappa Kappa Gamma, Lambda Pi Chi Sorority, Inc., Omega Phi Beta, Pi Beta Phi, Sigma Gamma Rho Sorority, Inc., Theta Nu Xi Multicultural Sorority, Inc., Zeta Phi Beta Sorority, Inc.

Selective Living Groups:
Brownstone (co-ed), Cleland (women), Languages (co-ed), Maxwell (co-ed), Mirecourt (co-ed), Prism (coed), Round Table (co-ed), Scott- Women's Studies (co-ed), SHARE (co-ed), Wayne Manor (men)

Governing Bodies:
Pan-Hellenic Association, National Pan-Hellenic Council, Latina Greek Organization, Inter-Greek Council, Inter-fraternity Council, Latino Greek Organization

Students Speak Out On...
Greek Life

> "Yeah, Greek Life pretty much dominates the social life here. Half of the girls are in sororities, and about one third of the guys are in fraternities. The social life outside the houses is pretty much dead."

Q "Freshman year, I went to a lot of the rush parties for frats and **found most of them to be filled with jerks**, so I skipped out on that. However, the frats are good for throwing parties. Most parties are open to everyone, so there's no need to be affiliated with any one group. Most of the sorority girls I know only do it for the mixers with the frats, so judge accordingly."

Q "Greek life here is actually fine. **I never thought I'd get involved in it, but I'm very glad I did.** There are no closed parties (except for formals and semi-formals), and there's no such thing as a guest list for frat parties. I don't feel like it dominates the social scene because you don't rush until second semester, so you have a chance to make friends before you're thrown into sorority life. I had friends ranging from all different types of sororities and independents."

Q "University officials are **starting to crack down on certain frat behaviors** that are deemed unsafe (such as some types of hazing) and have moved many from the main quad in order to make room for guaranteed sophomore housing."

Q "I was in a frat and really enjoyed it. **Frat parties aren't closed;** anyone can go to them, and they are almost always the ones throwing on-campus parties. But it's not essential to be involved in Greek life in order to have a social life."

Q "Perhaps it's big, but even though I'll never be Greek, **I'm not sure that's a bad thing**. Frats live in the dorms on campus, so all their parties are on campus and open. You can wander into any frat party you choose."

Q "**They're pushing all of the frat parties off-campus,** but they are all open, so you can go to whatever you like. I chose to stay independent, but I go to a bunch of sorority events. Rush is in the spring, so you wouldn't have to worry about that stuff until the second semester."

Q "Yes, **Greek life completely dominates the social scene**, but you don't have to be involved in it to go to their parties. Personally, I don't drink, so I usually only go out to frat parties once a weekend, but some people go Thursday, Friday, and Saturday. They can be really fun if there's dancing and you're with fun people, or they can be boring; it depends on which one and which night."

Q "Greeks dominate the social scene if you're into the party scene, although many people aren't into the party scene at Duke. **Greeks seem a bit segregated** and a little cocky, but I honestly do not have any negatives to report."

Q "Greek life is very big on campus. Sororities don't live together on campus, but **a lot of people join a fraternity or sorority.** Frat parties are one of the biggest forms of entertainment on the weekends, and I would definitely say that they dominate the social scene. However, I am unaffiliated, and I don't feel like that harms me socially in any way. I have some friends in frats and sororities and others who aren't, and I don't feel lonely or deprived because of my sorority-free life."

Q "The **frats aren't all stereotypical.** You're bound to find one whose parties you enjoy, if you enjoy parties at all."

Q "As for sororities, they don't live together and are basically large social clubs. If you like that, join one. I'm sure I don't own the 'right shoes' and couldn't ever bring myself to care anyway. So, while frat parties probably do dominate (there are some non-Greek selective houses who have parties), **there's no pressure to go Greek if you don't want to."**

Q "Duke has Greek life, but as I know it, **they don't dominate the social scene.** Since there are 5,000 undergrads, you can choose what to do."

The College Prowler Take On...
Greek Life

Greek life at Duke is honestly huge; not as huge as its basketball following, but huge nonetheless. You can survive socially without being a member, but you won't get through Duke without being at least somewhat affected by Duke's Greek scene. The number of students in fraternities or sororities might be a bit overwhelming at first (almost half the girls and about a third of the guys are in a sorority or fraternity) but it's easy to understand after a bit. Although a social life is possible without paying dues to some group, when so many students have given in and signed up, you look around and realize that you, too, want to belong and if paying some dues is the way to do it, it might be worth trying.

Don't be discouraged if you don't feel like joining some selective living group. It is quite possible to thrive at Duke without going Greek. However, you'll want to take Greek life into account when you're choosing a college. The cliques and groups can be wearing after a while, but other than a few bad apples, the Greeks here are quite friendly.

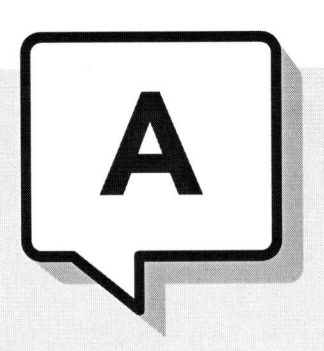

A

The College Prowler™ Grade on Greek Life: A

A high grade in Greek Life indicates that sororities and fraternities are not only present, but also active on campus. Other determining factors include the variety of houses available and the respect the Greek community receives from the rest of the campus.

Drug Scene

The Lowdown On...
Drug Scene

Most Prevalent Drugs on Campus:
Caffeine
Alcohol
Marijuana

Liquor-Related Referrals:
368

Liquor-Related Referrals from Residence Halls:
335

Liquor-Related Arrests:
4

Drug-Related Referrals:
43

Drug-Related Referrals from Residence Halls:
41

Drug-Related Arrests:
7

Drug CounselingPrograms:
Duke Student Health offers group and individual drug-and-alcohol programs.

Students Speak Out On...
Drug Scene

> "Alcohol is by far the most common drug of choice, and I think a lot of people take their drinking way too far. A few people smoke, and every once in a while I hear about someone with marijuana or something in a dorm room. I don't take part in any of that, though, so I don't know exactly what's going on."

Q "As far as drugs are concerned, whatever you want, you can get, but **prices are a little high.** The typical clientele are ignorant and have money to burn, so that kind of hurts everyone else."

Q **"A meth-lab was busted last year;** other than that I'm not sure."

Q "The drug scene is supposedly prevalent, but **I've never really seen it."**

Q "Students can avoid it, but if you're looking for drugs, **you're basically presented with a buffet** (if you know the right people). Marijuana is the most popular drug, and it can be found in most any social group."

Q **"Opium and Shrooms are available,** though on a limited scale and basis. Marijuana is popular here, and I believe that there are literally twenty people I could call on the spur of the moment should I want . . . ."

Q "The drug situation at Duke **isn't too big of a deal,** but the drug code of conduct is strictly adhered to."

Q **"There are lots of alcoholics** here, and that's the worst I've heard. Very little cigarette use, but it's there. There have been some ecstasy issues, but that's it."

Q "Alcohol is most definitely the drug of choice. **There's a weed presence,** but I'd say it's a distant second."

Q "I'm sure it's like most mainstream places: **if you're looking for it, you'll find it**. Otherwise though, it stays outside the mainstream, taking a much smaller second seat to alcohol (which is nearly everywhere)."

Q "Alcohol is the drug of choice, followed by **tobacco and marijuana.**"

Q "Drugs are illegal. Duke students are smart; thus they participate in illegal activities **behind closed doors.**"

The College Prowler Take On...
Drug Scene

The drug scene at Duke is pretty comfortable and not too pushy. If you want them, you can find them. If you don't, you shouldn't have to worry about it. Student responses reflect that most students are aware that there are drugs on campus, but no one seems threatened by it. It's almost impossible to get through college without a whiff of something grassy, but alcohol is more prevalent and widely used than any illegal substance. Of course alcohol plays a major role in the Duke social scene, but I dare you to find me a college where that's not the case (No, BYU doesn't count).

Since College Prowler grades on how pervasive the drug scene is, Duke gets reasonably high marks. Duke students can get through college with as much or as little drug use as they decide upon. There will always be the opportunity to use alcohol and drugs, especially if your group of friends uses them, but the pressure and prevalence of drug use shouldn't scare anyone away from Duke.

B

The College Prowler™ Grade on Drug Scene: B

A high grade in the Drug Scene indicates that drugs are not a noticeable part of campus life; drug use is not visible, and no pressure to use them seems to exist.

Campus Strictness

The Lowdown On...
Campus Strictness

What Are You Most Likely to Get Caught Doing on Campus?

- The Duke police department reports that it most commonly catches students vandalizing or drinking underage.

Students Speak Out On...
Campus Strictness

> "The campus is very strict with people about drugs. Drinking rules are very strict freshman year, and then they taper off after that. This is probably due to the fact that many Freshmen can't hang!"

Q "The cops actually aren't too bad here. They **mostly just observe outdoor parties** and make sure people are drinking from plastic cups and not bottles. They do, from time to time, raid rooms in an attempt to find drug offenders."

Q "**Campus police are strict** on East Campus, which is a dry campus. (Since it's the all-freshman area.)"

Q "The **police tend to look the other way at the parties on the West Campus** unless things get out of hand. Distribution of alcohol to underage persons must be done half-secretly though, as the resident assistants seem to be cracking down a bit. Near the end of school, the police searched the room of a guy they caught in a parking lot with fresh marijuana buds, and they found out he'd been growing it in his room, so obviously he's in trouble. I don't drink or do drugs, though, so I really don't know."

Q "Campus police are lax on drinking unless you're outside being stupid. **Don't drink in public on east campus**, keep that in your rooms; but you can drink pretty much anywhere on West. I know a few guys that smoke pot, and as far as I know, they haven't had any trouble."

Q "**Campus police are essentially a non-issue** when it comes to controlled substances. Students are rarely caught with drugs, and being cited for alcohol possession is quite rare."

Q "Campus police are much **more focused on preventing violent crime** and theft than on catching students for underage drinking. In all seriousness, in most locations on West Campus, I could smoke pot in the hall without having to worry about authority figures—although this doesn't mean that I recommend it!"

Q "Basically, they sit and watch at the frat parties to make sure no one gets hurt, but there's so much drinking that **there's not much that they can do**."

Q "**East Campus is a dry campus** since we're all freshmen, so I'd guess it's a lot stricter here. I don't know about drugs though."

Q "**Police are not all that strict** unless you're operating a twenty-four-hour bar out of your room or you set off the smoke detectors with your drugs. It seems like the norm is to drink freely, and do drugs (if you so desire) out of harm's way."

Q "Police at Duke are **not strict enough**."

Q "I see reports in the campus newspaper about the police citing people for underage drinking or having drugs in their dorm rooms, but I think **overall it's pretty loose**. Freshman and other under-twenty-one-year-olds don't seem to have any problem getting alcohol, and they almost never get in trouble."

Q "It usually depends on your RA. Drinking is part of the traditional social scene at Duke. For the most part, if you're smart, **police won't catch you.** They're not really patrolling the campus looking for drunken freshmen."

The College Prowler Take On...
Campus Strictness

Two words: food points. That's right, kids, Duke's food services will let you buy alcohol with your leftover food points from your meal plan, (when you're twenty-one, of course). The police usually leave kids alone when it comes to drinking and drugs, and the same goes for the university. Although students are occasionally caught doing unlawful things, police aren't likely to jump out from behind the sofa as you lift that plastic cup for your first guilty sip. So, unless your RA is scared for his/her job and shuts you down, you should be fine on campus.

The police in Durham have bigger things to worry about then kids getting drunk, so they're very lenient. RA's may turn you in, but you can easily figure out where they draw the line. At Duke, they're the most worrisome authority figures you'll have to deal with.

B+

The College Prowler™ Grade on
Campus Strictness: B+

A high Campus Strictness grade implies an overall lenient atmosphere; police and RAs are fairly tolerant, and the administration's rules are flexible.

Parking

The Lowdown On...
Parking

Student Parking Lot?
Yes

Freshman Allowed to Park?
Yes

Duke Parking Services:

Parking and Transportation Services
2010 Campus Drive
P.O. Box 90644
Phone: (919) 684-2201
Fax: (919) 684-8612

aux03.auxserv.duke.edu/parking/

Good Luck Getting a Parking Spot Here:

Anywhere close to the building you want to be in, especially on West. Duke does, apparently, have parking, but finding the places are difficult, and it's a trek from the parking lot to your dorm or class. An exception might be East Campus, where the parking lots are all pretty close.

Common Parking Tickets:

Expired Meter in Pay lot: $20
No Parking Area/Not Designated for Parking: $100
Handicapped Zone/Access Area: $250 (max)
Fire Lane: $200
No Permit/Expired Permit: $40.00
Landscape/Sidewalk/Pedestrian Way: $100.00
Service Space or Loading Area: $50
Reserved Space (including Visitor space): $20
Improper Permit: $40
Fraud Permit: $200
Improper Display: $10
Boot Fee: $50
Event Parking Violation: $100
Towing: $75

Parking Permits:

All students enrolled in classes for the fall semester are eligible to purchase and receive a parking permit for that academic year. Annual parking permits are sold based on eligibility and space availability in lots or zones. Parking permits can be purchased online or from the Parking and Transportation office.

Did You Know?

Best Places to Find a Parking Spot:

- **East Campus** usually has spots open—but that's only helpful if you live or go to class on East Campus.

Students Speak Out On...
Parking

> "Parking is a problem here, especially if you're worried about the safety of your car. Your most convenient parking will probably be right behind your dorm freshman year."

Q "The **lots on West are much more scattered,** and it's tough to tell where your permit is actually valid. The campus police will ticket you if you look at them funny. They'll also ticket your parents if they come to take you home at the end of the year. I guess I think there's a great deal of room for improvement in this area."

Q "Parking is a strike against Duke. **Parking has gotten really bad lately**, but compared to other schools (especially large public schools), it's not bad at all."

Q "Parking? Ha. That's kind of funny. You should be able to park your car, but **don't plan on driving to classes that are a little out of the way.** The student lots accommodate everyone, but on-campus parking is a pain."

Q **"Parking is adequate** here. They sell permits, and you park in a designated area. I don't know if residents have to pay extra for permits or not."

Q "It's horrible! There is **no legal parking anywhere.** I'd say there is currently enough parking to accommodate five percent of the Duke student population. They give parking tickets like crazy because everyone has no choice but to park illegally. You don't need a car until senior year."

Q "**Parking is a chore**, with few spaces on East Campus and cops who are always ready to give you a ticket."

Q "**Parking is one of Duke students' biggest gripes.** I don't have a car, so I don't remember how much permits cost, but I'm pretty sure they're rather expensive. It's not too hard to park on East Campus, as there are usually enough spaces, but you have to be careful not to park in the mysterious forbidden zones, which are sometimes not well-marked and result in tickets."

Q "**Duke police love to give tickets**. Parking on West Campus is absurd, but I think they're working on a parking garage or something."

Q "Parking is **horrible on West Campus,** but they are starting on a parking garage. It should be finished in a few years."

Q "Parking is **one of the low points on Duke's campus.** East campus parking spots are hard to find and may require a walk to your residence, depending on which one it is. Parking tickets are $30, $50, and $100, and are handed out generously."

Q "Parking is reserved to **very distant lots on campus.** Work is being done on the problem and they just built a new parking garage, but I'm unsure what effect that will have."

Q "Parking at Duke is horrible. It's very hard to find a parking spot, and it seems like **they're taking away more parking spots** as they do more construction."

Q "Parking seems terrible most of the year. East Campus has the only parking lots that are marginally convenient for students. **Parking on west campus involves a five-mile hike** that most students will experience on their first day, when they're relegated to the 'Blue Zone' for orientation."

The College Prowler Take On...
Parking

Duke doesn't have great parking. You might even be tempted to say parking sucks. You would certainly be within your rights to say so. But what university does manage to fit thousands of parking spots behind dorms and classrooms while maintaining the beauty of a campus? It is tempting to chalk up and criticize Duke's poor planning in regards to the terrible state of parking on campus. After all, Duke took out some old parking lots to add new buildings, which any fool can tell you will not help the parking situation. At times, students get so frustrated that parking illegally right in the middle of the traffic circle really doesn't sound like a bad idea. However, Duke has been working assiduously on a new parking garage in hopes of helping the situation. Even so, bringing a car is not necessarily the best way to go.

Parking is mentioned again and again as one of Duke's weak points. The fact that every student who goes to Duke automatically qualifies for parking is a bit disturbing—do they actually know how many people they are promising spaces to? If you decide not to come to Duke simply because of the parking situation . . . well then, we probably won't miss you. However, if you do decide to come you should know about the situation before hand.

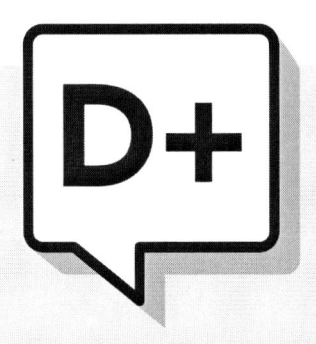

D+

The College Prowler™ Grade on

A high grade in this section indicates that parking is both available and affordable, and that parking enforcement isn't overly severe.

Transportation

The Lowdown On...
Transportation

Ways to Get Around Town

Taxi cab
Average cost of a cab from RDU International Airport to Downtown Durham, $29-$30

Durham Area Transit Authority (DATA)
Average cost 75 cents and 35 cents for people under 18 or 65 + (transfers are free).

Triangle Transit
Triangle Transit has a distance-based fare system, where the farther you travel, the more you pay. $1.50 to $2.00.

On Campus

Duke University Transportation
712 Wilkerson Avenue,
Durham, N.C. 27701-2864
Phone: (919) 684-2218

Duke provides a number of Bus routes. For complete schedules: aux03.auxserv.duke.edu/parking/busschedules/campusbusschedules.htm

Public Transportation

Durham Area Transit Authority (DATA)
123 Vivian St.
Durham, NC 27702
Phone: (919)687-7055

Triangle Transit Authority (TTA)
PO Box 13797
Research Triangle Park, NC 27709
Phone: (919) 549-999
http://www.ridetta.org/

Taxi Cabs

Hope Transportation Taxi
Phone: (919) 599-1881

Dixon Cab Co.
Phone: (919) 688-9593

Durham & Raleigh Taxi Cab Co.
Phone: (919) 688-6121

Airport Direct Taxi
Phone: (919) 688-7572

Durham's Best Cab Co.
Phone: (919) 680-3330

ABC Cab Co.
Phone: (919) 682-0437

Johnny's Taxi
Phone: (919) 682-8294

Car Rentals

Alamo, local: (919) 840-0132 ; national: (800) 327-9633, www.alamo.com

Avis, local: (919) 840-4750; reservations: (800) 831-2847, www.avis.com

Budget, local: (919) 840-4775; reservations: (800) 527-0700, www.budget.com

Dollar, local: (866)-434-2226; reservations: (800) 800-4000, www.dollar.com

Enterprise, local: (919) 840-9555; reservations: (800) 736-8222, www.enterprise.com

Hertz, local: (919) 840-4875; reservations: (800) 654-3131, www.hertz.com

National, local: (919) 840-4350; reservations: (800) 227-7368, www.nationalcar.com

Thrifty, local: (919) 832-9381; reservations: (800) 847-4389, www.thrifty.com

Triangle, local: (919) 840-3400; reservations: (800) 643-7368, www.trianglerentacar.com

Ways to Get Out of Town:

Airlines Serving Raleigh/Durham:

Air Canada, Fax: 1-866-584-0380 (403) 569-5333, www.aircanada.ca/

AirTran, 1-800-AIRTRAN (1-800-247-8726), www.airtran.com/

America West, (800) 327-7810, www.americawest.com

Continental, (800) 523-3273, http://www.continental.com

Delta, (800) 221-1212, www.delta-air.com

Northwest, (800) 225-2525, www.nwa.com

Skyway, (800) 452-2022 www1.midwestexpress.com/corporate/aboutSkyway/default.asp

Southwest, (800) 435-9792, www.southwest.com

United, (800) 241-6522, http://www.united.com

US Airways, (800) 428-4322, www.usairways.com

American Airlines, (800) 433-7300, www.americanairlines.com

Airport:

Raleigh-Durham International Airport

www.rdu.com/

Airport Authority Administration phone: (919) 840-2100

Information Desk: (919) 840-2123

The Raleigh-Durham International Airport (RDU) is approximately sixteen miles from Duke campus, or about twenty-one minutes driving

How to Get There:

Get a ride from a friend

Take a taxi

Take a Duke shuttle—before and after holidays, Duke offers free to shuttles to the airport, leaving from the east and west campus bus stops.

A Cab Ride to the Airport Costs: about $25

Greyhound

The nearest Greyhound station is only about half a mile from Duke's East campus.

For schedule information, call (800) 231-2222 or visit www.greyhound.com

Durham Greyhound Station:

820 W Morgan St
Durham, NC
27701-2043 US
Phone: 919-687-4800

Amtrak

The Amtrak station is also close to Duke campus—about a mile and a half away.

For schedule information, call (800) USA-RAIL (872-7245) or visit http://www.amtrak.com

Durham Amtrak Station:
400 W. Chapel Hill Street
Durham, NC 27701

Travel Agents:

Travel Agents International
201 S. Estes Drive
Chapel Hill, NC 27514
Phone: (919) 967-1123
Fax: (919) 933-0466

Travel Agents of the Carolinas
1101 Oberlin Rd
Raleigh, NC 27605
Phone: (919) 821-9800

Travelinks
2515 Hwy. 54 East Bldg.
Durham, NC 27713
Phone: (919) 484-2800
Fax: (919) 484-2810

Did You Know?

Best Ways to Get Around Town:
- Bum a ride from a friend
- Invest in a bike or a scooter
- Walk
- Take a bus—they're not the best, but they'll do.

If you want to get to Chapel Hill:
Take the Roberrtson Scholars Bus which goes directly from the West Campus bus stop to UNC campus. For more information, check: www.robertsonscholars.org/bus/

Students Speak Out On...
Transportation

> "Duke U. Transit runs buses back and forth between East and West Campus every few minutes. Getting a spot can be tricky between classes."

Q "The university transportation **isn't that bad**, at least it's not filthy or slow like Durham's."

Q **"Public transportation sucks** here. I suggest bringing a car, but good luck parking!"

Q **"Duke has a good transportation system** between campuses and through the University. I don't know about Durham's transportation system."

Q "There's a bus system, but you don't want to go to Durham. **Duke has its own buses that run between campuses,** and there's usually a free shuttle to the airport at the beginning of breaks; that's probably the only place you'll need to go."

Q "It's better to stay on campus if you don't have a car. **On campus transportation is very good.** I never used general public transportation. The airport is twenty minutes away. It gives you good connections to everywhere in the United States. Amtrak and Greyhound are also available."

Q "The buses are wonderful during the daytime and **awful during the weekends and evenings,** so it just depends on if you get to the bus stop at the right time then. The most I've ever had to wait was fifteen to twenty minutes."

Q "Durham was **very close to cutting all public bus services** before receiving a federal grant this summer. Have a car if you want to get around town. Campus transportation is for the most part convenient and prompt."

Q "The **campus buses are convenient,** but the Durham public transportation is awful. There are few routes, and they are usually not going where you want to go. This is not really a problem for the Duke students, though. There really isn't any need to go anywhere in Durham, so it doesn't matter that they can't get there. The campus really is their own little city for four years."

Q "I've never used public transportation. **The transportation from West/East is convenient and useful**. That's all that matters."

Q "I've never used public transportation, and I doubt many other Duke students have. **The campus system is good and usually reliable.** There is also a bus that runs from Duke to UNC regularly."

Q "Public transportation is **terribly inconvenient and expensive.** However, companies off-campus are slowly trickling in to remedy this problem. For example, a van will now take students to anywhere in the RDU area for a named price. However, I'm not sure how reliable this service is."

Q "I think that the Durham Area Transportation Authority runs buses near East Campus, but **I don't think that much of anyone ever uses them.** Most people travel by their own cars or friends' cars. That would be my recommendation because I've heard that the buses aren't very safe."

The College Prowler Take On...
Transportation

Duke's own campus transportation system is well run, extremely safe, clean, and efficient. Some of the bus drivers are obviously not excited about driving around a bunch of rich kids on the same route day after day, but who can blame them? The Durham system is another matter. If (having ignored all the best advice) you venture into Durham on the buses, we will not be responsible for you or your whereabouts thereafter. Please, please wait for a friend.

Most students carpool or take a taxi if they need to get to the airport. Many take the Robertson Scholars bus or have a friend drive them if they want to get to Chapel Hill. For movies and restaurants, students normally walk or take their cars. Durham, certainly isn't known for it's fast and efficient transportation system. However, if you're feeling desperate, brave, or just plain dumb, go ahead and give it a try.

The College Prowler™ Grade on
Transportation: B-

A high grade for Transportation indicates that campus buses, public buses, cabs and rental cars are readily available and affordable. Other determining factors include proximity to an airport and the necessity of transportation.

Weather

The Lowdown On...
Weather

Average Temperature
Fall: 60°F
Winter: 41°F
Spring: 59°F
Summer: 77°F

Average Precipitation
Fall: 3.82 in.
Winter: 3.86 in.
Spring: 4.23 in.
Summer: 4.11 in.

Students Speak Out On...
Weather

> "Weather here is seasonal but not extreme. I personally like it very much. You get all four seasons, but the winter is tolerable to outside activities (not like Utah, New York, or Minnesota)."

Q "You need **warm weather clothes from late October to early November** through about mid-late March, and one or two heavy coats and a hat wouldn't hurt for the few really cold weeks in January and February. Late August through October is summer-like, keep a light sweater handy in October; April is seventy all the time, and you're out by the time the unbearably hot weather comes in June. Bring an umbrella, because when it rains, it takes its time before it stops."

Q "The weather is usually **pretty mild here.** We have a few cold days, some rain, and then mainly really hot and muggy periods in the summer."

Q "Weather here is pretty great, for the most part, but it's **very inconsistent.** You have to check the weather; you can't just dress in something similar to what you wore the previous day."

Q "The weather is wonderful here. **Summers are mild to hot and winters do get cold.** We get snow during the wintertime. I think Durham averages eight inches of snow a year."

Q "The weather is perfect, and I'm not biased! **It doesn't really get cold.** It snowed only a few times during the winter, and it's usually not too hot unless you're just moving in."

Q "The weather from August to early November is typical summer weather. After that, the weather becomes colder, with usually one snowfall. **It starts to warm up during March."**

Q "**North Carolina weather is insane.** In the spring semester, you'll have weeks of forty-degree temperatures and rain followed by a week of eighty-degree temperatures and sunshine. The first few months of the fall semester are usually really nice, and the campus quads are like public beaches with some serious eye-candy."

Q "It's North Carolina weather, which means **it's impossible to predict.** It will get down to freezing in the winter, but not much lower, and not for long. Just as soon as you think it's warming up, it makes you get out the sweaters again. Still, it's nice for most of the time we're at school."

Q "During summer break, **it's often very hot and humid**, but as soon as school starts, the weather gets better."

Q **"It's extremely hot when you arriv**e and then it tends to be a nice seventy degrees the rest of the fall. Last winter was especially cold, but you can expect fairly mild conditions even in the wintertime."

Q "It's not as bad as you think when you move in during August! **The first few weeks are blazing hot,** but the weather calms down during the fall and becomes very comfortable. Winters are fairly mild, but it does snow at least once a year. Leave the heavy jacket at home, take a variety of cold and warm clothing, and enjoy some time outside – it's an absolutely beautiful campus."

Q "Weather here is really nice. **The fall and spring are long and pleasant.** Winter is short and mild. Summer is hot and humid. Bring everything, you'll need it."

Q "The climate here is fickle. **One day it's cold, one day it's hot.** It's definitely very hot in the summer and can get pretty cold in the winter. Bring a mixture of clothing, especially stuff that you can layer."

Q **"The weather is moody** in Durham. August, September, and April are sweltering. Every day in between is a toss-up between the most gorgeous and most miserable days ever."

Q "The weather is usually quite nice, although recently there has been an abnormal amount of rainfall. Shorts and short sleeves or tank tops are best until mid-October, and then long pants and sweaters are better until March or so. The winters don't usually get too cold, but **you'll need a heavy coat of some sort.** After all, walking is the main way to get to class, and you don't want to freeze on the way!"

Q **"Durham usually has wonderful weather.** The winters can be pretty mild (although Mother Nature was a little off this year). There are times when you can break out your flip flops as early as February. (Don't believe me? Just ask the class of 2005)."

The College Prowler Take On...
Weather

The weather in Durham is a lot of things, but predictable is not one of them. On the whole, it's very pleasant, but temperatures and conditions can swing from the high end of the scale to the low end with little warning. We're kind of like Mother Nature's little freak experiment. Bring your entire wardrobe! It's very humid, which is an indicator of some unbearably hot days, and some long, long rainy weeks (and months) when many students start wondering what it would be like if Duke hadn't put their drains on high ground and they could walk home without getting wet to the shins. Bring your galoshes! It also gets cold. There's not always a lot of snow, but you will regret it if you don't bring a nice warm coat.

At Duke, you're more likely to be concerned about heat stroke than frostbite, but be prepared for both (and everything in between). Remember, though, that in between the extremes, Duke has some days that are breathtakingly beautiful. Don't forget your sunglasses and bathing suits!

B

The College Prowler™ Grade on
Weather: B

A high Weather grade designates that temperatures are mild and rarely reach extremes, that the campus tends to be sunny rather than rainy, and that weather is fairly consistent rather than unpredictable.

DUKE UNIVERSITY
Report Card Summary

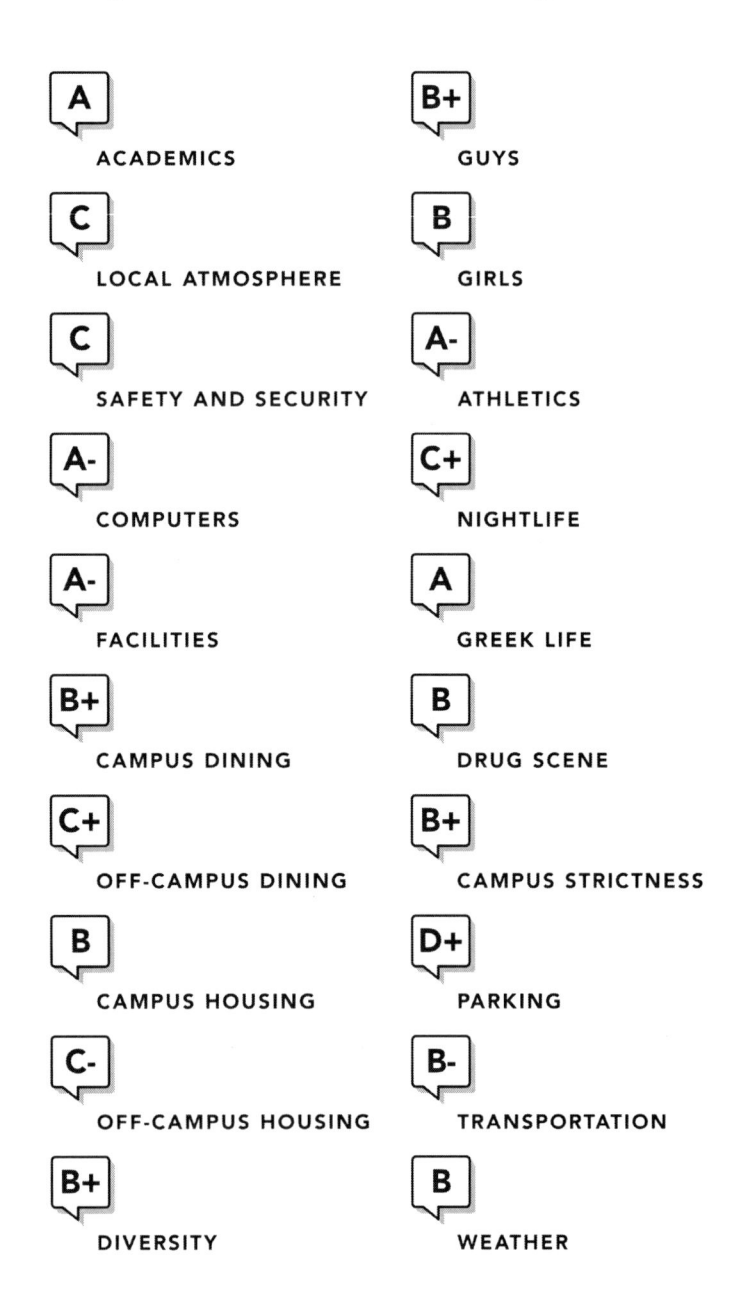

A	ACADEMICS	**B+**	GUYS
C	LOCAL ATMOSPHERE	**B**	GIRLS
C	SAFETY AND SECURITY	**A-**	ATHLETICS
A-	COMPUTERS	**C+**	NIGHTLIFE
A-	FACILITIES	**A**	GREEK LIFE
B+	CAMPUS DINING	**B**	DRUG SCENE
C+	OFF-CAMPUS DINING	**B+**	CAMPUS STRICTNESS
B	CAMPUS HOUSING	**D+**	PARKING
C-	OFF-CAMPUS HOUSING	**B-**	TRANSPORTATION
B+	DIVERSITY	**B**	WEATHER

Overall Experience

Students Speak Out On...
Overall Experience

"Duke is great; I find that the academic life is demanding but awesome in nearly every way: the professors, the classes, the dedication of the students. I love having been able to meet people from all over the world with diverse backgrounds, and I'm most happy with my decision to attend Duke."

"It was a good college experience. **Duke is a lot of fun**. I certainly have my gripes about the administration and the policies the university forces on students, but everyone says 'the grass is always greener on the other side.'"

"I honestly **would not mind being somewhere else**. There are other schools that are just as good, but I'm having a pretty good time anyway."

Q "If you get lucky like I did and accidentally wind up with a great bunch of crazy people as friends, **you'll have the time of your life**. All the academic stuff is pretty much irrelevant; college is about making friends and enjoying life."

Q "So far **the experience has been positive**. The worst part for me has been leaving friends and family behind, but I make an effort to keep in touch and to visit when I can."

Q "**Duke is great**. I'm glad I went, and I can't possibly imagine enjoying college as much anywhere else."

Q "I would never go anywhere else after having been at Duke this past year. Though I had my gripes about not getting into Harvard or MIT, I'm over that now. **Duke offers a great educational opportunity,** especially for undergraduates, and if you can take advantage of the Freshman Focus program, do so. It's a great program for your first semester."

Q "I'm glad I went to Duke; my overall experience has been really good. I wish I would have worked a little harder freshman year, but that's it. **If you want to be a well-rounded student, I'd say go to Duke**. We emphasize working hard, staying in shape, and partying hard."

Q "I came into this experience with very high expectations, and even so, I've been completely blown away. **The Duke student philosophy is 'work hard, play hard**,' and we do. Duke offers students the chance to tailor their experience to whatever it is that they're looking for. Duke offers an environment where students are surrounded by success. The drive to succeed is key to Duke students' success."

Q "I love Duke. I have no regrets. **The campus is unbelievably beautiful**, the teachers are great, and the people are incredible. What else could a kid ask for?"

Q "I love my school. **I would never want to be anywhere else**. I hope you come here and find that you love it as much as I do."

Q " Under the guise of providing students with a 'safe, diverse, and unique experience,' **the University has succeeded only in driving the social scene in a more covert, exclusive and potentially dangerous direction**. By dressing in baggy attire and hiding behind tipped baseball caps, are undercover deans attending on-campus parties to protect students, or to single them out and punish them? By dissolving selective living groups for late paperwork during final exams, by failing to return time-sensitive phone calls, and by refusing to work toward compromise in the reinstatement and housing process, are University officials more concerned with maintaining campus diversity, or with permanently removing social organizations? I'm not sure that this is a place you'll want to be in years to come."

Q "Duke's competitive advantage used to be that it was **'the coolest smart school in the country**.' Students who cared just as much about their experience outside the classroom had an incentive to choose Duke over the other top schools. Now, however, as the administration continues to push its own agenda without responding directly to student concerns, there is little to no incentive for the brightest, most well-balanced high school students in the country to choose Duke over any other Ivy League institution with a comparably dull, elitist social experience. In trying to become a 'me too' university, Duke is losing its competitive advantage, dropping from a first choice school to a fallback for the nation's top students."

Q "During my four years here, the thought that **I would like to be somewhere else certainly crossed my mind** more than once. After graduating, I'm glad I stuck with it, despite the homogeneity and conformity on campus."

Q "It's been a good experience. The professors are good, and the other students in my department are friendly. **There's nothing to do in Durham**, but I don't have time for anything anyway. Also, the cost of living is low."

Q **"I absolutely love Duke and everything about it!** I love the atmosphere, the classes, the professors, the people, and the whole college experience."

Q "I have loved Duke from my first visit as a high school senior, and I love it more each year. **I've never wished I were somewhere else**."

Q "I love Duke! I had such a great experience freshman year! **I was challenged academically,** had lots of opportunities to learn more about my field and future education/career, met so many really cool people, was able to form some very strong friendships, got to go to numerous basketball games and live in K-Ville, etc. I wish I were at Duke right now."

Q "I love Duke. The university is quite attractive from a visitor's standpoint, but I think **a lot of it depends on what you make of it yourself**. Sometimes, I wish that I had made other decisions, but how can you not? A lot of students turned down other big opportunities to come here. Enjoying Duke (or any college, I suppose) is about accepting the prestige and life you have at present and creating possibilities for your future."

Q "I've had a very positive experience at Duke so far. Once I adjusted to being away from home, **I made some really great friends**, and I like most of my classes. Plus, the campus is beautiful, especially the Duke Chapel, and I still find myself in awe of it sometimes. It's hard being away from my family and my boyfriend, who goes to Rice University in Houston, Texas, but I'm getting a great education in both academics and life. I don't have any wish to be somewhere else."

The College Prowler Take On...
Overall Experience

Duke students are generally happy with their experience, but it's not impossible to find students who imagine they'd be happier somewhere else. Academics, friendships, and even the beauty of the campus make this school an easy choice for many. However, a lot of students are concerned about the top-down social programming they see coming from Duke's administration. Rather than starting their own initiatives, Duke undergrads often seem apathetic and the administration, frantic to see things not only progressing, but progressing in the direction they see fit, tries to shove social programming down students' throats. Students and administration are still trying to find the balance of power and a unified direction. University politics have become a big concern, but the friendships students have forged seem to make up for whatever shortcomings they might perceive.

Duke is one of the top academic schools in the country, but that's not its hook. You'll never see Harvard's basketball team in the Final Four, or Yale students camping out for a week to get sports tickets. Obviously, basketball shouldn't be your major concern in choosing a college, but it is often used as an example because it typifies the difference between Duke and so many of the other top colleges. There's an emphasis on friends, social life, and fun here, and it's important to consider these aspects as well as academics when you're choosing a school. Remember, you're choosing the place you'll spend the next four years of your life, not just the name that shows up on your degree at the end.

The Inside Scoop

The Lowdown On...
The Inside Scoop

DUKE Slang

The BC: The Bryan Center

Blocking: In the housing lottery, it is possible to sign up in a "block." Students who block are given consecutive lottery numbers to have a better chance of getting rooms next to or near each other.

Cameron Crazies: What Duke students morph into once they enter Cameron Indoor Stadium.

The 'Dillo: Armadillo Grill. A popular place for some good Mexican food.

Grace: When the temperature dips below freezing K-Ville, campers are granted "grace" and allowed to head back home for the rest of the night.

Graffiti Bridge: The bridge between West and East on which students are allowed to plug parties, activities, theme weeks, etc.

Gross Chem: This is not really slang. The building is the "Paul M. Gross Chemical Laboratory Building," but is referred to as "Gross Chem"

K-Ville: Krzyzewski-ville. The village of tents created by avid students camping out for Duke basketball tickets.

Linking: After Freshman year, Duke students have the option of "linking" to a quad on west campus. Each east campus dorm is "linked" to a West campus quad.

Tent check: There are random tent checks for those who do tent for games, to make sure everyone's there. Someone's got to be there to answer the call. The killers are the 2 a.m. tent checks when everyone stumbles into the bitter cold in their pajamas.

Tunneling: East campus has a tunnel system under the dorms.

Walk-up line: The line of people who didn't camp out for the basketball games.

The WEL: West-Edens Link. This is the newer buildings and dorms which links west campus with Edens quad.

Things I Wish I Knew Before Coming to DUKE:

- How big the Greek life and drinking scene is (It's Huge)
- Parking can be very difficult
- Duke is pretty much its own little world—except on weekends, you don't really see the outside on this enclosed campus
- Durham is really not a great college town—Chapel Hill, however, passes quite nicely and is a free bus ride away
- Just because the Marketplace is all you can eat doesn't mean you should eat all you can
- It just might be worth it to get a doctor's note saying that you must have air conditioning

Tips to Succeed at DUKE:

- Meet as many people from as many backgrounds as you can. All the resources are there, whether you are looking for an intellectual conversation or help with a research project.
- Go to office hours! Many professors are willing to help, or even just to chat.
- Get a good amount of sleep, use the exercise facilities (because they're awesome) eat well, take care of yourself—you're mom isn't here to remind you of all that.
- Study. If you're looking to do well here, you're going to have to start studying some time.

DUKE Urban Legends:

- The only reason US News doesn't rank Duke ahead of Stanford is because Stanford would refuse to participate in the rankings if it was ranked below Duke.
- Nannerl O. Keohane (Duke's president) is really a man. (She's actually a lovely woman, we promise.)
- James B. Duke offered his endowment to Princeton University if its trustees would change the name to Duke. They refused. Trinity College agreed. Therefore, we are Duke University. (Other versions substitute Yale or Georgetown for Princeton.)
- East campus wall is ten feet high—three feet above ground and seven beneath
- All students, before they graduate, must complete four "graduation requirements." These include: tunneling, climbing atop Baldwin Auditorium, driving around the West campus traffic circle backwards, and "hooking up" with a freshman in Duke Gardens.

School Spirit:

Duke spirit centers around the basketball season, and during the Spring people are so avidly into Duke it's amazing. A lot of people at Duke seem to be bitter that they didn't get into an Ivy League school, and it's people like this who make Duke a little less pleasant. However, Duke does have some amazing rallying points if you allow yourself to get sucked in. Just don't be too standoffish and cosmopolitan; don't be afraid to try new things. Belonging to and rejoicing in a great college can be truly rewarding.

Traditions:

The Sower - There is a statue of a man on East Campus sowing seeds. The Sower is an old Duke tradition. At a time when women students were permitted only three dates a week and those were carefully defined, students could stroll about certain areas of campus without it counting as a "date". The Sower acquired the role of cupid as couples began placing pennies in his hand and claiming a kiss from their partner if the pennies were gone upon return. Although unnecessary today, it is not uncommon to still discover pennies in The Sower's hand.

Traditions (Continued...)

Midnight Breakfast - A rather recent tradition is much enjoyed on East Campus. The Sunday night before exams begin, freshmen line up on the quad to get into the Midnight Breakfast. Inside is a mixture of desserts and breakfast food, as well as (usually) some free t-shirts. This is definitely a tradition worth taking part in.

Blue Devil Mascot - The Blue Devil mascot appears to pump people up at all the basketball games. Since he can't talk to mock (and what's a basketball game without jeering?), he wears a headband with some little witticism about the other team. He also runs over to the band and bangs the bass drum during tip-off.

K-Ville - This little tent community has become highly organized in recent years, and Duke administration rather likes to have it to point to as an example of Duke's "coolness." Duke students still line up to get into it, though. It requires registration, scheduling, tent checks, and sitting for long hours in the bitter cold. However, there are some perks—free pizzas, meeting the basketball players, and some pretty darn good basketball seats.

Bonfires - After Duke beats UNC in a home game (which, of course, Duke has been known to do), Duke students run over to West campus to light stuff on fire—namely, dorm benches and old newspapers. Pledging Frat brothers may be charged with the task of guarding the frat bench from marauders looking for more firewood, but there is still plenty of wood left to go around. Duke administration has taken the precaution of getting fire permits, designating bonfire pits, and having firemen on hand before the burning times, which somewhat diminishes the fun and spontaneity of West Campus burning through the night, but does increase safety.

Last Day of Classes Concert - On the last day of classes Duke, like some other colleges, has a band come in to do a concert before finals begin. The bands are usually quite good, and it's a great chance to go hang out and relax with friends before you have to bury yourself in your room and glare at them if they interrupt your studying.

Finding a Job or Internship

The Lowdown On...
Finding a Job or Internship

The Lowdown:

Finding jobs and internships can be a harrowing experience for everyone. For some people things just fall into place. Others really have to work at it. Don't trust that you'll be one for whom things will fall into place—get in touch with the career center. They offer résumé help, mailing lists, job listings, etc. It might help, and it sure won't hurt.

Advice:

Go to the job fair at the beginning of the school year, go to subsequent job fairs and job forums, get the résumé help, get in contact with the career center, get on the mailing lists, apply for the internships. Be proactive. Job fairs are usually held in the student center.

Career Center Resources & Services:

career.studentaffairs.duke.edu/

110 Page Building

P.O. Box 90950

Durham, NC 27708

Phone: (919) 660-1050

Fax: (919) 684-4999 ~ Help: (919) 660-1070

Hours: Monday, Thursday, & Friday 9 a.m.-5 p.m., Tuesday & Wednesday 9 a.m.-7 p.m.

Alumni Services:

- BlueDevilTRAK: Job Postings and OCI information
- DukeSource: Offers the ability to network with Duke Alumni
- Internship Exchange: Lists summer opportunities
- E-leads: Shows unique job leads online
- Email lists: sign up to get information about job openings in careers of your choice.
- Career Article: monthly article on hot career topics
- Brochures & Guides for students and employers
- Resource room in 217 Page

Alumni

The Lowdown On...
Alumni

Website:

Website: www.dukealumni.com

Duke Office of Alumni Affairs

614 Chapel Drive

Box 90572

Durham, NC 27708-0572

Phone: (919) 684-5114 or (800) FOR DUKE

Fax: (919) 684-6022

Email: kay.ladd@daa.duke.edu

Services Available:

Online Alumni Directory

Lifetime Email Service

DAA Calendars

Career Services & Networking

Alumni Library

Duke Visa Card

Alumni Admissions Advisory Forum

Major Alumni Events:

Duke Alumni are invited to participate in all sorts of events. The yearly homecoming and Reunion are probably the biggest events. Homecoming has a whole slew of related events scheduled for the weekend, and Duke supplies car rental discounts, and so on, for returning alumni. The alumni association also offers helpful resources for those who are planning on coming to the reunions, such as airline information, airport shuttle service information, and rental car information. There are also a number of events planned for each reunion, including the Big Dance, held in a tent on main West quad.

Alumni Publications:

Duke Magazine

The magazine started in 1984, and is mailed out six times each year, in the second month listed on the cover banner. Duke seniors receive it free of charge during their last year on campus and for two years after that; graduate and professional-school alumni receive it for one year after their graduations. The magazine reaches about 75,000 readers annually! Alumni receive the magazine if they pay the yearly subscription fee ($15; $30 foreign), if they pay the annual Duke Alumni Association dues, or if they contribute at a certain level to the Annual Fund.

Did You Know?

Famous Duke Alumni:

- Richard M. Nixon, Robert Richardson, Judy Woodruff, Annabeth Gish, Kelly Goldsmith, Kevin Gray, Grant Hill, Christian Laettner, Nancy Hogshead, Jim Spanarkel, Jay Bilas, Mike Gminski, and John Feinstein

Student Organizations

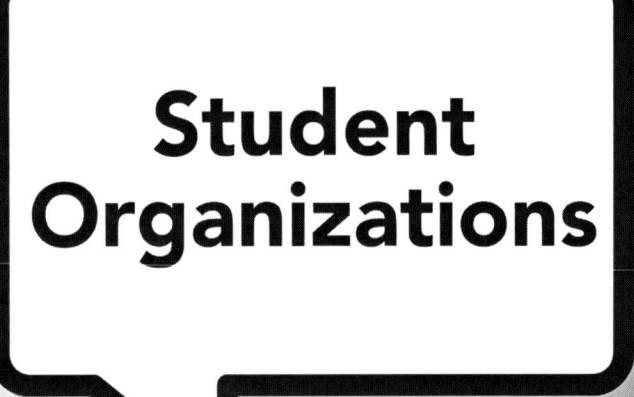

Student Governments:

Duke Student Government - DSG (undergraduate)
Engineering Student Government - ESG (undergraduate)
Graduate and Professional Student Council - GPSC

Clubs, living groups, and other organizations:

For a complete listing of all organizations or for links to student group websites, visit http://www.duke.edu/org/org.html

AIESEC
Air Force ROTC
AQUA Duke (Alliance of Queer Undergraduates At Duke)
American Red Cross Club
ASCE (American Society of Civil Engineers)
Arab Students Organization
Army ROTC

- Arts Theme House
- Asian Students Association
- Association for Computing Machinery
- Association for India's Development
- Ballroom Dance Club
- BASES (Building Awareness through Shared ExperienceS)
- Biomedical Engineering Society
- Black Pre-Health Organization
- Black Student Alliance
- Borrowed & Blue
- The Brass Ring
- Broadway at Duke
- Brownstone
- Cable 13
- Cambridge Christian Fellowship
- Campus Crusade for Christ
- CAMU - Cultural Anthropology Majors' Union
- Canterbury Dorm
- Catholic Student Center
- CHANCE tutoring program
- The Chanticleer
- Chess Club
- Chinese Folk Dance Club
- Chinese Students and Scholars Association
- Christian Medical and Dental Society
- The Chronicle
- Circle K International
- Cleland House
- Community Service Center
- Cook (Samuel DuBois) Society
- Craft Center
- Defining Movement
- DELTA Smart House Project
- DevilNet

Diya (South Asian-American Association)
DRAGO (Duke Role-Playing and Gaming Organization)
Duke-Durham Hunger Alliance
East Campus Council
Environmental Alliance
Episcopal Center
Falun Dafa Cultivation Group
Freeman Center for Jewish Life (FCJL)
Global Grasp
Graduate and Professional Student Council - GPSC
Graduate and Professional Women's Network
Graduate Student Dance Club
Habitat for Humanity
Hillel
Hindu Students Council
Hoof 'n' Horn
Imago Dei
Inter-Collegiate Auto Racing
International Association
InterVarsity Christian Fellowship
Intramural and Sports Clubs
Investment Club-Student Run Money
Karate Club
Korean Student Association
Lady Blue
Latent Image
La Unidad Latina
LEAPS
Linux Users Group
Local Colour
Lutheran Campus Ministry
Manna Christian Fellowship
Mathematics Union
Maxwell House

- Men's Club Tennis Team
- Mi Gente: Asociacion de Estudiantes Latinos
- Mountain Biking At Duke
- Music Exchange
- Muslim Student Association
- National Association for the Advancement of Colored People
- National Society of Black Engineers
- Navy ROTC
- Out of the Blue
- Outing Club
- Pan-Hellenic Association
- Photogroup
- The Pitchforks of Duke University
- Psychology Majors' Union
- PreMed Society
- PRISM: The Multicultural Selective Living Group
- Project BUILD
- Project WILD
- Radiology Interest Group (RIG)
- Robotics Club
- The Round Table
- Rugby Football Club (Men's)
- Rugby Football Club (Women's)
- Samuel DuBois Cook Society
- Safe Haven
- Self Knowledge Symposium
- S.H.A.R.E. living group
- Shotokan Karate Club
- Singapore Students Association
- SOCA (Students of the Caribbean Association)
- Speak of the Devil
- SpeakOUT!
- Student Action with Farmworkers
- Students of the World

- Taiwanese Student Association
- Tae Kwon Do Sports Club
- Turkish Student Association
- Ultimate Frisbee Club
- Unitarian Universalist Community
- Visual Arts
- VOICES Magazine
- Water Ski Club
- Wayne Manor
- Wesley Fellowship
- Westminster Presbyterian Fellowship
- Wilderness Outdoor Opportunities for Durham Students (WOODS)
- Women in Science and Engineering
- Women's Center
- WXDU

The Best & The Worst

The Ten BEST Things About Duke University:

1. Caring Professors
2. College Hoops Baby!
3. The Student Body
4. Wireless Internet
5. Duke Chapel
6. Unlimited Meal Plan
7. Stoic Buildings
8. Ethnic Diversity
9. Random Duke Statues
10. The Pleasant Weather (Especially the Fall)

The Ten WORST Things About Duke University:

1. Kids who didn't get into Harvard.
2. High-school-style cliques
3. Administration organizing spontaneity
4. Three straight weeks of rain
5. Communal showers
6. No A/C!
7. Loafers and pink shorts
8. Catching the bus
9. Student officers who don't show up to their own events
10. No Parking! Anywhere!

Websites you might find interesting:
www.duke.edu/TSA/life_at_Duke/trivia.htm
www.triangle.citysearch.com/
www.soulofamerica.com/cityfldr/durham13.html
www.duke.edu/web/police/
www.healthydevil.studentaffairs.duke.edu

Visiting DUKE

The Lowdown On...
Visiting Duke

To Schedule a Group Information Session or Interview:

Interviews: Although interviews are not required, they will assist you in learning more about life at Duke.

Please call 4-6 weeks in advance of a proposed campus visit.

Group Information Sessions: The admissions staff will give you an overview of Duke. Contact the Office of Undergraduate Admissions (919-684-3214).

Website:
www.duke.edu/about/visiting.html

Walking Tours:

No appointment is necessary. For groups larger than 10, contact our office in advance. Call ahead at (919) 684-3214 if you require accommodations or assistance.

Special Group Tours:

There are special walking tours of the campus for groups with more than ten and fewer than fifty students. Special tours are available to groups of high school age students only. Call (919) 684-3214 several weeks in advance. .

Overnight Visits:

To arrange to spend a night on campus contact a current student through the Student Locator Service at (919)684-3322. Or call the Student Hosting Office at (919) 684-3214.

Visiting a Class:

While there is no pre-registration required to attend one of the classes, it's a good idea to arrive early and notify the professor you would like to observe his or her class.

For Schedules, visit www.duke.edu/web/ug-admissions/visit/tours.htm

HOTEL INFORMATION

Brookwood Inn Durham
2306 Elba Street
Durham, North Carolina
Phone: (919) 286-3111

Campus Arms Motel Apartments
2222 Elba St
Durham, NC 27705
Phone: (919) 286-9133

Days Inn Durham
3460 Hillsborough Rd,
Durham, NC 27705
Phone: (919) 383-1551

Fairfield Inn Durham
3710 Hillsborough Road
Durham, NC 27705
Phone: (919) 382-3388

Hampton Inn Durham
1816 Hillandale Road
Durham, NC 27705
Phone: (919) 471-6100

Hilton Durham Hotel
3800 Hillsborough Road
Durham, NC 27705-2328
Phone: (919) 383-8033

Holiday Inn Express
2516 Guess Road
Durham, NC 27705
Phone: (919) 313-3244

Howard Johnson Inn – Durham
1800 Hillandale Road
Durham, NC 27705
Phone: (919) 477-7381

Inkeeper Durham West
3454 Hillsborough Road
Durham, NC 27705
Phone: (919) 309-0037

Millennium Hotel Durham
2800 Campus Walk Avenue
Durham, NC 27705-4479
Phone: (919) 383-8575

Red Roof Inn
1915 North Pointe Drive
Durham, NC 27705
Phone: (919) 471-9882

Super 8 Motel
2337 Guess Road
Durham, NC 27705
Phone: (919) 286-7746

The University Inn
502 Elf St
Durham, NC 27705
Phone: (919) 286-4421

The Washington Duke Inn & Golf Club
3001 Cameron Blvd
Durham, NC 27705
Phone: (919) 490-0999

DIRECTIONS TO DUKE CAMPUS DRIVE:
From Greensboro and Points West:
- Via 1-85 North: Exit onto N.C. 147 (Durham Freeway).
- Take first exit off Durham Freeway onto 15-501 S. toward Chapel Hill.
- Stay in right lane, take second exit (#107), marked Duke Univ. West Campus, to N.C. 751.
- At fourth traffic light (Duke University Rd.) take a left. Continue past Wannamaker Dr., Towerview Rd. and Edens Dr. (not marked) to Chapel Dr.
- Turn left onto Chapel Dr. at large stone pillars. Continue to traffic circle and take circle around to First St., which is Campus Dr.

DIRECTIONS TO DUKE CAMPUS DRIVE (*Continued...*)**:**
From Richmond and Points North:
- Via I-85 South: In Durham, take the left-lane exit (#174B) for US 15-501 South Bypass Duke University/Chapel Hill.
- Cont. on U.S. 15-501 to 4th exit (#107), Duke U. West Campus, right-lane exit N.C. 751.
- Turn left onto N.C. 751 S., go under the freeway.
- At fourth traffic light (Duke University Rd.) take a left. Continue past Wannamaker Dr., Towerview Rd. and Edens Dr. (not marked) to Chapel Dr.
- Turn left onto Chapel Dr. at large stone pillars. Continue to traffic circle and take circle around to First St., which is Campus Dr.

From RDU Airport, Raleigh and Points East:
- Via I-40 West: Exit onto the Durham Freeway (N.C. 147). Take Durham Freeway to Chapel Hill St. Exit (#13).
- Take right on Chapel Hill St. Continue straight on Chapel Hill St. until it turns into Duke University Rd. Cross Anderson St. to Chapel Dr.
- Turn right on Chapel Dr. at large stone pillars. Continue to traffic circle and take circle around to First St., which is Campus Dr.

From Chapel Hill:
- Via US. 15-501 North. Take 15-501 North, marked Duke Univ./Med Ctr. Do not take 15-501 Business.
- Take exit for N.C. 751 (#107) marked Duke University West Campus.
- Turn right onto N.C. 751 S. (Cameron Blvd.).
- At third traffic light (Duke University Rd.) take a left. Continue past Wannamaker Dr., Towerview Rd. and Edens Dr. (not marked) to Chapel Dr. Turn left on Chapel Dr. at large stone pillars. Continue to traffic circle and take circle around to First St., which is Campus Dr.

Words to Know

Academic Probation – A student can receive this if they fail to keep up with their school's academic minimums. Those who are unable to improve their grades after receiving this warning can possibly face dismissal.

Beer Pong / Beirut – A drinking game with numerous cups of beer arranged in a particular pattern on each side of a table. The goal is to get a ping pong ball into one of the opponent's cups by throwing the ball or hitting it with a paddle. If the ball lands in a cup, the opponent is required to drink the beer.

Bid – An invitation from a fraternity or sorority to pledge their specific house.

Blue-Light Phone – Brightly-colored phone posts with a blue light bulb on top. These phones exist for security purposes and are located at various outside locations around most campuses. If a student has an emergency or is feeling endangered, they can pick up one of these phones (free of charge) to connect with campus police or an escort service.

Campus Police – Policemen who are specifically assigned to a given institution. Campus police are not regular city officers; they are employed by the university in a full-time capacity.

Club Sports – A level of sports that falls somewhere between varsity and intramural. If a student is unable to commit to a varsity team but has a lot of passion for athletics, a club sport could be a better, less intense option. If a club sport still requires too much commitment, intramurals often involve no traveling and a lot less time.

Cocaine – An illegal drug. Also known as "coke" or "blow," cocaine often resembles a white crystalline or powdery substance. It is highly addictive and dangerous.

Common Application – An application that students can use to apply to multiple schools.

Course Registration – The time when a student selects what courses they would like for the upcoming quarter or semester. Prior to registration, it is best to have an idea of several back-up courses in case a particular class becomes full. If a course is full, a student can place themselves on the waitlist, although this still does not guarantee entry.

Division Athletics – Athletics range from Division I to Division III. Division IA is the most competitive, while Division III is considered to be the least competitive.

Dorm – Short for dormitory, a dorm is an on-campus housing facility. Dorms can provide a range of options from suite-style rooms to more communal options that include shared bathrooms. Most first-year students live in dorms. Some upperclassmen who wish to stay on campus also choose this option.

Early Action – A way to apply to a school and get an early acceptance response without a binding commitment. This is a system that is becoming less and less available.

Early Decision – An option that students should use only if they are positive that a place is their dream school. If a student applies to a school using the early decision option and is admitted, they are required and bound to attend that university. Admission rates are usually higher with early decision students because the school knows that a student is making them their first choice.

Ecstasy – An illegal drug. Also known as "E" or "X," ecstasy looks like a pill and most resembles an aspirin. Considered a party drug, ecstasy is very dangerous and can be deadly.

Ethernet – An extremely fast internet connection that is usually available in most university-owned residence halls. To use an Ethernet connection properly, a student will need a network card and cable for their computer.

Fake ID – A counterfeit identification card that contains false information. Most commonly, students get fake IDs and change their birthdates so that they appear to be older than 21 (of legal drinking age). Even though it is illegal, many college students have fake IDs in hopes of purchasing alcohol or getting into bars.

Frosh – Slang for "freshmen."

Hazing – Initiation rituals that must be completed for membership into some fraternities or sororities. Numerous universities have outlawed hazing due to its degrading or dangerous requirements.

Sports (IMs): A popular, and usually free, student activity where students create teams and compete against other groups for fun. These sports vary in competitiveness and can include a range of activities—everything from billiards to water polo. IM sports are a great way to meet people with similar interests.

Keg – Officially called a half barrel, a keg contains roughly 200 12-ounce servings of beer and is often found at college parties.

LSD – An illegal drug. Also known as acid, this hallucinogenic drug most commonly resembles a tab of paper.

Marijuana – An illegal drug. Also known as weed or pot; besides alcohol, marijuana is one of the most commonly-found drugs on campuses across the country.

Major – The focal point of a student's college studies; a specific topic that is studied for a degree. Examples of majors include physics, English, history, computer science, economics, business, and music. Many students decide on a specific major before arriving on campus, while others are simply "undecided" and figure it out later. Those who are extremely interested in two areas can also choose to double major.

Meal Block – The equivalent of one meal. Students on a "meal plan" usually receive a fixed number of meals per week.

Each meal, or "block," can be redeemed at the school's dining facilities in place of cash. More often than not, if a student fails to use their weekly allotment of meal blocks, they will be forfeited.

Minor – An additional focal point in a student's education. Often serving as a compliment or addition to a student's main area of focus, a minor has fewer requirements and prerequisites to fulfill than a major. Minors are not required for graduation from most schools; however some students who want to further explore many different interests choose to have both a major and a minor.

Mushrooms – An illegal drug. Also known as "shrooms," this drug looks like regular mushrooms but are extremely hallucinogenic.

Off-Campus Housing – Housing from a particular landlord or rental group that is not affiliated with the university. Depending on the college, off-campus housing can range from extremely popular to non-existent. Those students who choose to live off campus are typically given more freedom, but they also have to deal with things such as possible subletting scenarios, furniture, and bills. In addition to these factors, rental prices and distance often affect a student's decision to move off campus.

Office Hours – Time that teachers set aside for students who have questions about the coursework. Office hours are a good place for students to go over any problems and to show interest in the subject material.

Pledging – The time after a student has gone through rush, received a bid, and has chosen a particular fraternity or sorority they would like to join. Pledging usually lasts anywhere from one to two semesters. Once the pledging period is complete and a particular student has done everything that is required to become a member, they are considered a brother or sister. If a fraternity or a sorority would decide to "haze" a group of students, these initiation rituals would take place during the pledging period.

Private Institution – A school that does not use taxpayers dollars to help subsidize education costs. Private schools typically cost more than public schools and are usually smaller.

Prof – Slang for "professor."

Public Institution – A school that uses taxpayers dollars to help subsidize education costs. Public schools are often a good value for in-state residents and tend to be larger than most private colleges.

Quarter System (sometimes referred to as the Trimester System): A type of academic calendar system. In this setup, students take classes for three academic periods. The first quarter usually starts in late September or early October and concludes right before Christmas. The second quarter usually starts around early to mid–January and finishes up around March or April. The last quarter, or "third quarter," usually starts in late March or early April and finishes up in late May or Mid-June. The fourth quarter is summer. The major difference between the quarter system and semester system is that students take more courses but with less coverage.

RA (Resident Assistant): A student leader who is assigned to a particular floor in a dormitory in order to help to the other students who live there. A RA's duties include ensuring student safety and providing guidance or assistance wherever possible.

Recitation – An extension of a specific course; a "review" session of sorts. Because some classes are so large, recitations offer a setting with fewer students where students can ask questions and get help from professors or TAs in a more personalized environment. As a result, it is common for most large lecture classes to be supplemented with recitations.

Rolling Admissions – A form of admissions. Most commonly found at public institutions, schools with this type of policy continue to accept students throughout the year until their class sizes are met. For example, some schools begin accepting students as early as December and will continue to do so until April or May.

Room and Board – This is typically the combined cost of a university-owned room and a meal plan.

Room Draw/Housing Lottery – A common way to pick on-campus room assignments for the following year. If a student decides to remain in university-owned housing, they are assigned a unique number that, along with seniority, is used to choose their new rooms for the next year.

Rush – The period in which students can meet the brothers and sisters of a particular chapter and find out if a given fraternity or sorority is right for them. Rushing a fraternity or a sorority is not a requirement at any school. The goal of rush is to give students who are serious about pledging a feel for what to expect.

Semester System – The most common type of academic calendar system at college campuses. This setup typically includes two semesters in a given school year. The "fall" semester starts around the end of August or early September and finishes right before winter vacation. The "spring" semester usually starts in mid-January and ends around late April or May.

Student Center/Rec Center/Student Union – A common area on campus that often contains study areas, recreation facilities, and eateries. This building is often a good place to meet up with fellow students and is most commonly used as a hangout. Depending on the school, the student center can have a huge role or a non-existent role in campus life.

Student ID – A university-issued photo ID that serves as a student's key to many different functions within an institution. Some schools require students to show these cards in order to get into dorms, libraries, cafeterias, and other facilities. In addition to storing meal plan information, in some cases, a student ID can actually work as a debit card and allow students to purchase things from bookstores or local shops.

Suite – A type of dorm room. Unlike other places that have communal bathrooms that are shared by the entire floor, a suite has a private bathroom. Suite-style dorm rooms can house anywhere from two to ten students.

TA (Teacher's Assistant): An undergraduate or grad student who helps in some manner with a specific course. In some cases, a TA will teach a class, assist a professor, grade assignments, or conduct office hours.

Undergraduate – A student who is in the process of studying for their Bachelor (college) degree.tent role in campus life.

Notes

Notes

Notes

Notes

Notes

Notes

Notes

Notes

Need More Help?

Do you have more questions about this school? Can't find a certain statistic? College Prowler is here to help. We are the best source of college information on the planet. We have a network of thousands of students who can get the latest information on any school to you ASAP. E-mail us at *info@collegeprowler.com* with your college-related questions. It's like having an older sibling show you the ropes!

Email Us Your College-Related Questions!

Check out **www.collegeprowler.com** for more details.
1.800.290.2682

COLLEGE PROWLER™

Notes

Tell Us What Life Is Really Like At Your School!

Have you ever wanted to let people know what your school is really like? Now's your chance to help millions of high school students choose the right school.

Let your voice be heard and win cash and prizes!

Check out **www.collegeprowler.com** for more info!

COLLEGE PROWLER

Notes

Do You Have What It Takes To Get Admitted?

The College Prowler Road to College Counseling Program is here. An admissions officer will review your candidacy at the school of your choice and create a 12+ page personal admission plan. We rate your credentials with the same criteria used by school admissions committees. We assess your strengths and weaknesses and create a plan of action that makes a difference.

Check out **www.collegeprowler.com** or call 1.800.290.2682 for complete details.

COLLEGE PROWLER™

Notes

Pros and Cons

Still can't figure out if this is the right school for you? You've already read through this in-depth guide; why not list the pros and cons? It will really help with narrowing down your decision and determining whether or not this school is right for you.

Pros	Cons

COLLEGE PROWLER

Notes

Need Help Paying For School?
Apply for our Scholarship!

College Prowler awards thousands of dollars a year to students who compose the best essays. E-mail *scholarship@collegeprowler.com* for more information, or call 1.800.290.2682.

Apply now at **www.collegeprowler.com**

COLLEGE PROWLER™

Notes

Get Paid To Rep Your City!

Make money for college!

Earn cash by telling your friends about College Prowler!

Excellent Pay + Incentives + Bonuses

Compete with reps across the nation for cash bonuses

Gain marketing and communication skills

Build your resume and gain work experience for future career opportunities

Flexible work hours; make your own schedule

Opportunities for advancement

Contact *sales@collegeprowler.com*
Apply now at **www.collegeprowler.com**

COLLEGE PROWLER™

Notes

Do You Own A Website?

Would you like to be an affiliate of one of the fastest-growing companies in the publishing industry? Our web affiliates generate a significant income based on customers whom they refer to our website. Start making some cash now! Contact *sales@collegeprowler.com* for more information or call 1.800.290.2682

Apply now at **www.collegeprowler.com**

Notes

Reach A Market Of Over 24 Million People.

Advertising with College Prowler will provide you with an environment in which your message will be read and respected. Place your message in a College Prowler guidebook, and let us start bringing long-lasting customers to you. We deliver high-quality ads in color or black-and-white throughout our guidebooks.

Contact Joey Rahimi
joey@collegeprowler.com
412.697.1391
1.800.290.2682

Check out **www.collegeprowler.com** for more info.

COLLEGE PROWLER™

Notes

Write For Us!
Get Published! Voice Your Opinion.

Writing a College Prowler guidebook is both fun and rewarding; our open-ended format allows your own creativity free reign. Our writers have been featured in national newspapers and have seen their names in bookstores across the country. Now is your chance to break into the publishing industry with one of the country's fastest-growing publishers!

Apply now at **www.collegeprowler.com**

Contact *editor@collegeprowler.com* or call 1.800.290.2682 for more details.

COLLEGE PROWLER

Notes